Anonymous

Tell your Wife

Anonymous

Tell your Wife

ISBN/EAN: 9783337715182

Printed in Europe, USA, Canada, Australia, Japan

Cover: Foto ©Thomas Meinert / pixelio.de

More available books at **www.hansebooks.com**

BOSTON
LEE AND SHEPARD, PUBLISHERS
NEW YORK
CHARLES T. DILLINGHAM
1886

COPYRIGHT, 1885,
BY LEE AND SHEPARD.

All rights reserved.

TELL YOUR WIFE.

TELL YOUR WIFE.

CHAPTER I.

*"Youth, Hope, and Trust,
These form a trinity that makes a heaven upon earth."*

"O HARRY! it was splendid!"
     That was Hester.
"Old fellow, you did well!"
"You'll eat your dinner with an appetite, after that triumph!"
"The dean spoke very favorably. He's rather sparing of his compliments, you know."

So said one and another of a class of thirty, as after the valedictory, which had cost me much pains and close study, I came down from my pedestal, and mingled with the crowd.

Even the wheezy professor, Hester's father, with his chin on his chest, condescended to smile his approbation, and even to essay a complimentary sentence.

But what cared I for them all, with Hester's slim white hand in mine? Hester's brown eyes worshipful, Hester's smile making my heaven? Now very soon I could claim her for my wife. I had loved her since the first day I entered the college, and she, a shy girl of fourteen, had looked up at me with a smile in her soft brown eyes. She was then fourteen: now she was seventeen, my bonny Hester.

"So you liked it," I said, with natural and perhaps pardonable exultation. "Well, I don't mind telling you that I thought it pretty good myself — before I reached the platform; but, while delivering it, it seemed flat, stale, unprofitable."

"I never would have dreamed it. You seemed quite lost in the subject," she made reply. "How did you like the flowers?"

"Charming — although I did not examine them critically. I left them on the desk. Jenkins will attend to them."

"I'm afraid you don't like flowers," Hester said, with an incipient pout.

"Because I sent them away? I don't mind telling you that I don't like carrying a bouquet, though I adore flowers. If ever I have a church, I mean to keep the altar supplied, in season and out.

"'There grows a flower on every bough:
 Its gay leaves kiss — I'll show you how.'"

Hester laughed.

"You'll please wait till you get home," she said.

"Hester, have you tied your throat up?" asked Mrs. Vaughan, with awful dignity. "Mr. Clements, you quite astonished us. The professor says it was the best valedictory since the time of Tindell. But dear me! Tindell is in deacon's orders yet. He married too young, Mr. Clements. It was very wilful of him, very wrong. We all warned him."

Hester gave me a look that said, "Take care! beware!" and so spared her mother my opinion of early marriages.

The dear girl had just one little fault. It had sometimes occurred to me that she was a trifle too prone to take matters into her own hands,— vulgarly speaking, of "bossing." Her mother ruled the household, including the professor; that was evident on a brief acquaintance.

And yet the dear girl had a quick insight into things that sometimes puzzled her elders. She was electric, magnetic, and possessed of the ability to read human nature.

She read me, but I was not then aware of the fact; she read and yet loved me. Doubtless she wished in a degree to shape my future. This, I apprehend, was one of her most cherished ideas. She saw my enormous love of approbation; my desire to make all men, and women too, my friends. There was the possibility of a downfall from just this fact,—that I rated my gifts beyond their warrant, that I looked down upon the commonplace, and my vanity of race was simply stupendous. Sleeping in my heart of hearts was a pride, that, some day awaking, might spring upon me, and destroy me root and branch.

I had noticed her ability as well as inclination to rule. By the simple arrangement of putting on her embryonic attempts an arbitrary interpretation of my own, I had come to the conclusion, that in all respects, if she ever became my wife, she must defer to my judgment, not I to hers. This decision I never had the courage to put in words. She was so lovely, so lovable,— grace was attendant in all she did and said,— her utterances were so pure and noble, her interest in all I did so sincere, that I kept my resolution to myself, partly, perhaps, for fear that I should not be able to carry it out.

"You will come home with us to dinner, the professor says. Mr. Launce has done us the honor to accept our invitation," said Mrs. Vaughan, in her deep voice, that seemed to issue from the triple folds of her chin.

Launce was a slim, dignified dandy, the heir to hundreds of thousands.

Hester, who had taken my arm, gave it a little pinch. I knew exactly what it meant,— "What do I care for him, or his riches?"

He was in the parlor when we reached the professor's house, standing by the mantel, pinching his chin. He had that distinctive habit by which I should have known him in any part of the world. Slim, tolerably well shaped, with eyes that would easily have met but for the insignificant line that formed the bridge of his nose, a mouth of large proportions, a flat forehead, mutton-chop whiskers and a mustache, — two features which saved his face from utter vacuity, — he was a man incapable of attracting attention, save for his prospective millions. As it was, all the mothers were fishing for him, Mrs. Vaughan among them; and all the daughters — save Hester — dying to receive a smile from him.

Curiously enough, though Hester treated him almost with rudeness, he was more than willing to lay all his possessions at her feet.

"Oh! Mr. Launce!" said Hester indifferently. "Excuse me for a few moments — I'll be back soon, Hal," turning markedly to me; and away she tripped. I sauntered to the farther end of the room. Hope and love made me almost insolent.

Hester came down in a few moments radiant. Never had she seemed so beautiful. A gown of blue, laces like sea-foam at throat and wrist, her eyes shining, her lovely head with its wavy, rippling locks changing from bronze to gold, her merry smile, — was I some day to be the possessor of all those charms? The very thought made me shiver with a thrill of ecstasy. Am I talking nonsense? Every honest man in love will answer, No!

The memory of that day is burned in upon my brain. For me it was supreme from the moment I had achieved the first victory of my young manhood till I parted with Hester.

The professor always gave good dinners, but it was Hester's sparkling face I feasted on that day. She played the violin with rare precision and beauty if not with genius. Mr. Launce listened, simpered, and pinched his chin. He seemed to lack courage to speak to her while I was by. I fancied I held him dumb by a sort of mesmeric power.

That evening I talked with the professor. Before I knew it, almost, I had asked him for his daughter. He referred me to Mrs. Vaughan, who gave a decided refusal. I was too young; my income only enabled me to take care of myself. The professor contemplated a visit to Europe. He had relatives there. It was an opportunity for her darling that she dared not forego.

I listened as she droned on, my heart all one dumb ache. Never having counted upon a refusal, I was like a child just beginning to understand that he cannot have his own way. I protested. As well might one try to cut adamant with a pen-knife. Mrs. Vaughan's mind was made up, and she was granite-firm. Hester knew it when she saw me. In what way, I cannot conjecture, but she had dismissed Mr. Launce. I held her two hands, and she saw all the misery of my soul.

"I dreaded it would come to this; but don't you mind, Harry. I'll be true as steel."

"But — to be gone — a whole year!" If life had depended upon it, I could not keep back the tears. I am afraid they overran my eyes.

"It does seem a long time; but courage," said the high heart. And then the golden plaits of the high heart laid on my shoulder, and she was sobbing. It was not three minutes by the filigree clock on the mantel-piece, however. When she looked up, the soft eyes were defiant.

"She knows I love you — she knows she married papa when he was a poor student. She ought not to be my mother — but she is, and she knows we all obey her in this house. I won't run away with you, because that would be foolish, and wouldn't look respectable. Besides, you've got your orders to think of, and there's plenty of hard work before you. Come, now, I'll prophesy. Before the year is out, you will have your own church, marry some foolish girl "—

I stopped her speech with a kiss.

We sat together for a little space, then I left the house, more miserable than I had ever felt in my life, little thinking that I should not see her face again for many weary months.

CHAPTER II.

"Not to be true in seeming, is sometimes not to be true in fact."

HOW the year passed, I cannot tell. Occasionally came letters from friends who had met my darling; never one came to me from her — that was forbidden. Yet night and morning her sweet words comforted me, —

"Don't you mind, Harry. I will be true as steel."

I believed her. She would come home to me more beautiful than ever, she would come home of age, ready and willing to take the responsibilities of life in her own hands, hers and mine together.

Then came news. The professor had decided to remain another year. I was furious; for I had built up my plans, and every thing was contingent upon her coming.

There were those who would have consoled me, and I was sorely tempted. Men said that Miriam, Hester's cousin, was the most beautiful woman in the city; and Miriam always reminded me of Hester. Shall I tell of Miriam's weakness, and my thoughtless folly? The girl knew my love-history — Hester had confided in her; and yet — perhaps she thought, hoped, or longed, that, being so far away, Hester might forget me, or I her. Be that as it may, I formed the habit of going to her for sympathy. She was different from Hester in many ways, — more yielding, less aggressive, more intellectual. She lived with her parents in an unpretending house, not quite on the outskirts of the city, but far enough out to have a wilderness-garden of its own; and the porch with its old-fashioned lounging-chairs, and interlacing branches of rose-vines, was a very comfortable place.

The effect of my constant visits came to be evident in time. Miriam dressed for me, looked for me, and I was not blind to the fact. Here was my selfishness conspicuous. I could not give up my own comfort, and the comfort she gave me, though it might be to her hurt. I saw the changing color, the quick consciousness, the brightening of the face, as one who will not see though the fact be self-evident. I am afraid I enjoyed the knowledge, guilty as it made me feel, contemptible as it was.

One day when she was at the piano, singing, I spoke of the song as one nobody could sing exactly like Hester. She burst into tears, and left the room. All was revealed to me then.

For a week I kept aloof from the pretty home; for a week I was torn with doubts and fears. The girl had stirred my sympathies to such a degree, that, had I been assured that Hester had faltered once in her determination, I would have married Miriam.

When I met her, she looked pale, and her eye wandered. Her manner was colder and prouder, as if she had schooled herself to composure. She would not have pity. I saw that, and made no change in my manner. Her mother spoke of her fretfully; whether she half surmised what the trouble was, I could not tell. To hints I was impervious.

"I wish Miriam could have gone with Hester," she said one day impatiently. "I think her uncle might have taken her, though the outfit would have cost pa a year's profit. Still, it might have paid, Miriam is so beautiful! The child isn't well; something frets her; whether or not it is Hester's letters,—though that can't be; for I must say they are perfect pictures, and well worth being printed."

"She is enjoying the old country, then?" I said.

"Enjoying it! you ought to see Miriam's letters. Now in a palace, now in some great cathedral; pictures, statues, fountains; lords, ladies, balls, theatres, and parties, — I should think the child would die."

"Yet but just now you were saying that you wished Miriam had gone."

"Oh, well!" she colored, and cast a quick glance at me that seemed both angry and imploring. "Miriam is not such an enthusiast as her cousin — less excitable, and more even in her temperament, as you must sometimes observe. And then — yes, I do wish she had gone, poor child!"

I had taken up a book, conscious that her words conveyed a covert reproach. Was it that that angered me? or the fact that I had never seen one of those charming letters written by the hand of my dear, absent love? An unreasoning jealousy took possession of me. I began to rack my brain for some method by which I could get possession of them. In my course of self-instituted study, I was reading "Theodorus;" and, chameleon-like, my mind took the hue of his reasoning. In his moral scheme, there is no eternal difference between good and evil; and so insensibly do one's ideas take color from the quality of thought originated in a powerful and creative brain, that for the time I might have been his disciple without being aware of the delusion. Thus, why might I not practice a little guile for the better consummation of my object? All that remained to do was to set my wits to work, to come oftener to the cottage, to let myself bask in the smiles of Hester's cousin, and the work was done.

I protest I meant no harm, either in my cogitations or my intentions. I had been thrown in the society of women all my life. There were no boys in my mother's family. My twin was a girl, from whom I had scarcely ever concealed a thought, even in my college days. I had been trained by my sisters. Dolly, she who seemed flesh of my flesh, and for whose sake I had often said I would never marry, — until I met Hester, — pursued the same studies that I did up to my last year at college, when illness prevented her from keeping pace with me. I was always more at home with women than with men, always happier in their society.

Did the remembrance of my ministerial calling come to the rescue? Yes, more times than I can count. Yet I was still a man, and not yet aware of my own weakness. My reason had not outgrown its callow youth, and I was not then in the habit of making severe requisitions of my conscience.

The plan worked admirably. In a week or two Miriam was her arch, beautiful self, and I was drifting out into treacherous waters.

The color came back to her cheek, and the lustre to her eye. I thought I could ignore all my undoing at my will — which proves what an ignoramus he is who plans without reason. There are moments in a man's career that he never forgets. All through life, in one way or another, they will be brought back to him with photographic distinctness, — the careless thought, the idle action, even the unconsidered words.

"By your words you shall be justified, and by your words you shall be condemned, is a tremendous practical law," says an old writer. I believe it, for I have experienced the fact.

At last I had gained that point when I decided to ask Miriam to show me Hester's letters. I remember the afternoon when I locked my study-door, and set out for the cottage.

It was a pleasant walk; and all the outdoor world was a picture, high in light, beautiful in tints, rich in shadows. The sun shone softly on the old-fashioned houses standing inside of quaint gardens, for ours was a city not despoiled of nature's handiwork. Many fine old families there were who made their homes after the fashion of those their ancestors had left more than a century before; and every place one passed, whether protected by a modern iron fence, or only a well-kept hedge of living green, was a study for an artist. I could have fancied myself in some lovely old English town, so exactly were such features reproduced as walls covered with ivy; cool arbors, over-arched with elm and maple; curious latticed windows; massive porches; leafy coverts that led into labyrinthine walks; here a common, bright with grass, and clumps of bushes and well-grown trees; there a bit of rustic woods, filled with verdure of all colors, with thousands of sprays of ferns, and gray moss clinging to every thing; again, a mass of crumbling rocks, all their fissures aglow with treasures of bramble-blossoms, and wild-strawberry leaves, and a thousand dyes impossible to describe.

As I neared the little cottage where Miriam lived, my heart beat faster. I knew I should find her waiting for me, a happy smile on her lips; and I had told her I should ask a favor of her, though I had not enlightened her as to what its character was to be.

Did you ever succeed in convincing yourself that you were not meaning any harm, when in your very soul you knew you were walking on forbidden ground? If not, then you must have been born a saint.

I had called Miriam sister and cousin, but my actions challenged the hypocrisy.

CHAPTER III.

*"The dear old home, with orchards near
Of apple, plum, and downy peach."*

MIRIAM was waiting for me, just as I had fancied. A spray of apple-blooms at her throat made her seem an incarnation of the promised summer. The glow of cheek and throat was more vivid than I had ever noticed before; and as in dreamland we do incredible things, so in my waking dream the impression of her beauty was so vivid, that I held her hand until she herself withdrew it, blushing and confused.

"Will you sit here?" she asked, "or go inside? Is it too cool for you outdoors?"

It was all glare and sunshine here, albeit the vines did their best to soften the light. Preferring the shadow just then, I went inside the low-ceiled, comfortable parlor. I shall never forget it as it looked on my entrance. On the right and left of the fireplace stood immense vases, brought from China when the captain,

Miriam's father, was in the service. All the furniture was old-fashioned, and much worn, but in good repair. The uniform polish of the floor was broken by dainty rugs, all of them bought in foreign bazaars, and rich with the devices of Eastern looms. It was a place to rest in, and in which Miriam's beauty shone with tenfold lustre.

"See," said Miriam, when we were comfortably seated, "what a beautiful gift to-day's mail brought me." She held up a costly diamond ring which sparkled on the third finger of her left hand.

"People will say you are engaged," I said lightly. "It should be a rich lover would give you a ring like that."

"Can't you guess? Hester sent it," she continued, the glow fading from her face. "And in my letter is one for you; and, if you like, you are to see all the letters she has written me, so she says."

The visitation had fallen suddenly. I had been weeks industriously planning how I should consummate this matter, and here it was ready done to my hand. I suppose I looked my astonishment, for Miriam grew rosier yet.

"You don't seem so *very* glad," she said.

"No — I — that is, if you will pardon me, may I have my letter?"

"Oh, certainly!" she said, and went towards a writing-desk in the corner, took the letter therefrom, and handed it to me.

"Don't ask to be excused," she said; and her voice trembled a little. "Read it now, if you wish to. You must be anxious to hear from her."

"Since this is the first letter she has written me in fifteen months," I said, "I will take my time in reading it." And the missive seemed to burn me where I had thrust it, in my breast-pocket. I cannot tell what spirit possessed me, but I was kinder to the beautiful girl before me than I had ever been in my life. Perhaps it was because of a consciousness that it was the last time. I cannot remember that I was troubled with any qualms of conscience; they came afterward. I do not know that I purposely demoralized myself, — I think not; but I had gone so far that it seemed to matter not what further risks I ran.

I know I took home with me a face beautiful with hope, almost transfigured, in fact, and in thinking of which, my heart sank within me while I composed myself to read Hester's letter. Miriam had brought me a little packet tied with ribbon as I left, and I am afraid I called her "dear" when I thanked her.

In the privacy of my study I opened the letters, — first her own to me, in which I read her noble, lofty heart.

"I have come to the age of a maiden's liberty, Harry, and I shall begin a correspondence. If it does not seem graceful in me to take the initiative step, lay it to my unchanging love."

My cheeks burned as I read her innocent revelations. How nobly true she had been! What a heart was mine! Was I worthy of such affection?

"After this," the letter went on, "write me as often as you will. Mamma has made many plans for me, but to no purpose, and I think she has about given it up. We shall be here some months longer, and bring home some pretty things from the foreign bazaars; for papa has been prodigally generous, and I have spent a little money myself."

I sat down that night, and wrote twenty pages. All the fervor of my early love rushed over my heart, and in that fervor I wrote. How glad I was! how free, how happy, I felt!

Miriam's image faded out. I applied myself more diligently to my studies. I had passed a fair examination, and would soon be a full-fledged priest. I had now no longer an excuse to lead me to the house of Miriam. To tell the truth, I was thoroughly ashamed of myself when once I was in a situation to face my own treachery. I became magnanimous, and decided that I would not even call on Miriam again, more for her sake than mine. If I could but have seen what this decision was to cost me! I sent back Hester's letters with a note that I should be absent for several weeks on a visit to my sisters. My face grew hot while I was writing it. Oh, yes, I was very penitent! and all those long weeks Miriam lay in her bed raving with fever, nigh to death's door.

Meantime I had reached Myrtle Mount, the old homestead from under whose blessed roof I had followed father and mother to the grave out there in the little rustic garden of the dead at the west of the village church. Dolly was not yet quite recovered from a slight illness; but I heard her half laughingly, half sobbingly, call my name as I stepped over the well-worn portals. Another moment, and she was in my arms, very pale, but very happy. God had been good to me, I thought, in giving me so many blessings. This dear little girl, so graceful and lovely, with the beauty of soul irradiating every feature, had always been one with me, and I was her idol. How she had watched me, followed me, clung to me!

"We told her she was killing herself trying to keep up with you in Greek," said Anne, whose great black eyes beamed on me from under her first pair of spectacles; "and, sure enough, she came near it."

"Never mind! I'll make it up yet," said Dolly, an arm over my neck; and, as she spoke, she lifted the hair from my forehead, and kissed it again and again.

"You are prettier than ever," I said, taking the slight figure on my knee, while she lay in my arms like a little child. "I never saw your cheeks so red, or your eyes brighter."

Anne's eyes met mine, — she had laid aside the spectacles, — and there was a strange, earnest, yearning expression in her glance. Just then I remembered that our mother had died of consumption, beautiful to the last; and a great fear fell on my heart.

I forgot it, however, an hour after, when together we stood looking at the grand sunset, whose splendid Tyrian dyes rolled down the hills, followed by sheets of gold, and, as when we were children, we saw islands of silver in oceans of emerald, bordered by broad-branching palms a hundred feet high. The clamor of the wildfowl in the air, the distant music of cow-bells, the sweet fragrance of the hay, the far-off winding roads, and a glimpse of the river that threaded its serpentine coils through miles of verdure, — how they brought back the heart of the boy, till he forgot that the cares and trials of manhood were in his future!

"I have a letter from Hester in my pocket," I whispered, my arm round Dolly's slender waist.

"Is she coming home?" asked Dolly.

"I hope so, soon."

"I didn't know — I thought, maybe — you were tired of waiting, you know," she added, looking away.

"Oh, no, darling! she is worth waiting for," was my reply. "I will let you see her letter, but none of the rest. You are my second self, you know."

"I was till she came," was the answer; "but never mind, I have you a little while yet. Anne is calling me; they are too careful of me, but of course we must go in. To-morrow we'll have a romp as in the dear old times."

What change was there in my sweet little sister? She was like, yet unlike, the merry child she had always seemed, with all her wisdom.

We all sat round the open fire that night, the apples toasting on the hearth, and the quaint old mug full of sweet cider on the stand beside us.

"Have you any idea where you will be settled?" asked Anne, who sat next to me, knitting lace.

"There is a talk of my going to old St.

John's," I answered. "Of course I am too young for it, but they seem to have made up their minds. The salary is small, the parish large, and the church not over-rich; but I prefer to take it with all its drawbacks. I might be assistant rector of Trinity, with possibly a larger salary; but I like being my own master too well for that. One might as well take the responsibility at once."

"Yes, I think you are right," said Anne, who had been gazing thoughtfully at the fire. "And who is to be the new rector's wife?"

She never looked towards me, but plied her bright little needles.

"We heard it was Miss Miriam, old Captain Hope's handsome daughter," said Dora.

"What! heard that! away out here? Who on earth told you such nonsense?" I asked, feeling the blood rush to my face.

"We have friends, you know, in the city," said Belle, who was herself engaged to a lawyer, a man whom I thought well off, but seldom met.

"Templeton told you."

Belle shook her head.

"It was a woman, you might know," said Dolly sharply.

"Yes, it was a woman," said Anne; "and, by what she said, we had decided that you were off with the old love, and on with the new."

"Oh, nonsense!" I was nettled, but laughed.

"Yes, we really understood that you were engaged," said Dora.

"Don't marry any of them," said Dolly impulsively. "*I'll* keep house for you."

"I may call upon you sooner than you think," I said. "I preach my trial sermon on the thirtieth."

"Oh, it would be delightful if only I could!" said Dolly, her beautiful eyes sparkling.

"Yes, I believe she would leave us all," spoke up Anne, "and go to the ends of the earth with you."

"So I would, if he needed me," was the reply. "If only we two could go off as missionaries, I'd be willing to die for the cause. Then," she added, in an undertone, "you could get married."

I had no time to answer this with a little loving rebuke, as I intended; for Belle asked me to take up the apples, offering me a little pair of silver tongs used for that purpose.

"Is Miss Miriam so *very* beautiful?" queried Anne, her keen, questioning eyes looking straight in mine.

I knew my face was fever-red. I had not dreamed of being followed to this place by the ghost of my own indiscretion.

"She is a very handsome young lady," I said,

"but not nearly as lovely, in my eyes, as my promised wife, Hester Vaughan."

"How the gossips do talk!" said Belle angrily. "Here we have been suffering keenly on account of the scandal, as we thought it. Why, an old friend of mine was actually told that Miss Miriam Hope wore her engagement-ring, and that the wedding-day was fixed. It seemed to me that we might have received at least a hint of the proposed change."

"Of course you would," I said, knowing not what else to say. Did Miriam's reproachful eyes look at me out of the flame?

"Sister Anne, it seems to me you ought to tell brother Harry who was our informant," said Dora.

"Well, to be sure, the news came from a very ordinary source," said Anne, smiling; "though the woman is one of the members of St. John. Her husband is a tailor, and they have a whole houseful of children. Her name is Dickory; and the male Dickory makes clothes for Colonel Albright, our nearest neighbor,— has for years. This Mrs. Dickory, a very common woman, always brings them home; and she was our informant. I expect the male Dickory works also for Captain Hope, and that is how the news originated."

"Plague take the gossips!" I said; but all the

time there was a vigorous knocking at the door of my conscience, and I would have given worlds to undo the work of the past few months.

On the following day came the news of Miriam's illness, through the same informant. Anne met Mrs. Albright at the town-depot for gossip, — the store. They had put up prayers for her at St. John: there was very little hope of her life.

What my feelings were on receipt of this intelligence, I leave the reader to infer. All the poetry of my visit to the home of my fathers was blotted out. I felt myself her executioner, and it was a bitter thought that I must lack something of the qualities of true manhood in my own eyes. I returned to the city sooner than I should, dreading to hear the worst.

My fears were not realized. She was past the danger, and recovering slowly. I wrote my little sister the good news, together with the fact that I had accepted the office of rector of St. John; that the people had promised to build me a parsonage; and that, if Hester staid abroad another year, she should keep house for me till my bride came, and after that make her home with us.

CHAPTER IV.

"O Sorrow dark as death!
. . . that I had been
Thy veiled prophet."

THE first face I glanced at in my first service as rector of St. John was Miriam's.

Very pale she was, calm, cold, disdainful, and beautiful as a saint. It was some weeks before chance threw us together again. I held out my hand. For a moment her lip trembled, and her eye flashed. She seemed at first not willing to shake hands, but thought better of it.

"You are my pastor," she said; and the tone was an accusing one.

"And soon to hold a nearer relation," I said, quietly and firmly.

The blood surged up to her cheeks. For one moment there was an expression in her face that positively frightened me, it was so intense, so evil. It was gone almost as quickly as it came.

Her mother had been talking with a neighbor in the next pew. Now she came forward.

"Come, Miriam," she said, almost rudely.

"Is the captain well?" I asked, determined to be friendly.

"Thanks, no," she deigned to answer: "he has been ill ever since my daughter got up. He worried so over Miriam, I don't think he will ever be himself again. He's very fond of Mr. Lyon, who has administered spiritual consolation while you were away."

Mr. Lyon was the rector of St. James, — the most influential parish and church in the diocese, — but the captain was one of the oldest members of St. John. For a moment I felt the humiliation she counted upon. But why did they not all give up their pew at St. John, and go to St. James? I should have been better pleased, looking my own soul in the face. The sooner I forgot the past, the better, if I could; or if I could have felt sure that Miriam's feelings were altered towards me. Penitent enough, I was, but that would not undo the past. I felt sure, in the light of that experience, that I loved only Hester, that I could never have felt other than sentiments of admiration towards Miriam. The question was settled in my mind forever.

But what of Miriam? She had a certain power — a power to make me uncomfortable — to thrust herself upon my sermon-page, sometimes, to my indignation; for I had almost to wrestle with the inclination to look at her, study her, wonder of what she could be thinking, of how she regarded me.

The old captain died in less than a month, and now the faces of the two women deeply bordered in black demanded my sympathy more than ever. In that great trouble we seemed to be brought nearer together, to forget that there had been unkind thoughts, harsh judgment. Miriam grew more like her old self: her mother came to me for advice in her business affairs, as well as for pastoral comfort. The captain had not made much money, and of course they must depend more or less on their own exertions. There was enough to keep them for a time: the house belonged to them.

"Miriam might keep school," said Mrs. Hope, who possessed very little of the commodity her name implied; "but she is so delicate since her sickness, that I want to spare her if I can. She writes a beautiful hand: if there was any way, she might make a little money by her pen as a copyist or an amanuensis."

I promised to do my best. Quite sure by this time of Miriam's forgiveness, our relations assumed the old friendliness, if not the old familiarity. I went oftener to the cottage, but it was to consult with Mrs. Hope. When with Miriam, I felt like an intruder, fearful that I might, out of sheer nervousness, say or do something my conscience might not approve. I was cured of experimenting. I would not give it the plainer name of flirting, out of respect to my calling. Miriam seemed to me to be changed, more devout, more gentle. Only now and then, if I spoke of Hester, that strange expression that had so startled me once before would come into her face, and trouble me.

Meantime I continued to receive Hester's wonderful letters. The dear child opened all her heart to me, unfolded her treasures of travel so vividly that it enabled me to see with her eyes, and hear with her ears.

At last, the very night that the finishing-touch was put upon the parsonage, I received the letter that told of her intention to start on the following Tuesday. She must then be on the ocean. I could hardly rest, eat, or sleep. I sent the news in a note to the Hopes, and then schooled myself to wait. I passed the professor's house on my way to St. John. All the windows were open. Workmen were in the grounds, carpets on the lawn : all was in a state of bustle and activity through the mansion and the grounds. I was the happiest man alive. My love was coming back, as true to me as when she gave her last adieu. No doubt, she had met those who could and would have given her station and riches. How could she help but have admirers wherever she went?

I walked on air. All heaven and earth seemed to be keeping jubilee.

A black-robed figure met me. It was Miriam. A gentle pity stole into my heart in the midst of my rejoicing.

"You have heard good news," she said; and I thought her lip quivered.

"Yes: they are almost here," was my brief rejoinder.

"They? — you mean *she!*" was her response; but her voice was strained and harsh.

"Surely you will be glad to see her," I said, surprise nearly taking my breath away.

"No — I hate her! no — I hate every thing that is happy!" she rejoined.

"Then, Miriam, you hate me," I said.

"Yes, I do," she said, giving way to sudden passion. "You have wrecked my life, *and you know it!* You know it standing in that sacred desk; you know it in your moments of solitude; you will have the knowledge to make you still happier when *she* is your wife."

"Miriam," I said gently, offering my arm, "you must not stand here: you are trembling, angry, beside yourself. Let me take you home."

"No," she replied, gasping: "I don't need any help. I am going home by myself. I am wretched. I may have said too much, but I felt it all."

She saw perhaps the absolute horror in my face.

"I know what you think of me," she said rapidly, "but I don't care. I have wanted to tell you what I felt ever since my illness. Now, perhaps, my brain is giving way. I wish you would let me go." She put her hand to her head.

"The road is open," I said, stepping aside. She started forward, but walked so unsteadily I feared that she would fall. As for me, the whole round horizon had turned dark. Had I indeed wrecked her life? That was a grave charge to a man in my position. And Hester! What would she say did ever a knowledge of the fact come to her hearing? She would despise me, and yet I could lay my finger on no intentional evil deed.

This interview had completely demoralized me. I went home, and threw myself on the lounge in my study, her wild eyes and haggard face a haunting memory. Then I rose, and went to my desk. An unfinished sermon lay beside an open book; the lines, "*Man is his own worst enemy*," the last I had penned, staring me in the face.

I committed the deed of a madman. I wrote

mine enemy a letter, — a letter any innocent man might write, and yet be judged harshly by prejudiced minds in the reading.

All the next day passed. Towards night came a singular note.

"Please forget what I said. I have terrible headaches since my illness, and they nearly drive me distracted. *You are safe with me.* No one alive shall ever know what I have suffered, or have cause to distrust you.

"Respectfully,
"MIRIAM."

I read it again and again. What had I said in my letter? Written in the half-distracted mood in which I then was, I could not recall a sentence. I knew I had not turned state's evidence against myself. It seemed to me that I had written frankly, but at the same time cautiously. How could I dream that she would ever use that letter as a weapon against me?

For a day or two I was uneasy and nervous, but the feeling wore away.

Hester should never know of this one cloud that had darkened the serenity of my life. Why should she? I reasoned. She had, no doubt, leaned on other men's arms, looked into other eyes, perhaps unconsciously formed liking into love by their magnetic glances. I asked for no confessions, — neither did I, in my heart, believe she had done these things, — I would make none. Miriam's anger had worn itself out, — a merely selfish anger, a fierce protest against herself, and made against her will, so I chose to think.

That night Miriam sat in her pew: she did not often come on week nights. I had been having some trouble with the choir: my mind was wandering, and her face made me more helpless still. She sat there like a fate — the woman in black — perhaps a fixed hate in her heart for life. How I got through the services, I scarcely knew. I went home, and read all Hester's letters, and, in recalling her lovely presence, grew calmer and happier. Surely all would be right, when, that dear face near to mine, we sat together, and talked of the past, and looked forward to the future!

CHAPTER V.

*"A cottage home, a lowly place,
   Painted by vines and climbing roses,
   Nestled beyond a woodland space."*

"DEAREST Harry!"

With these words she greeted me, coming forward with hands outstretched, with eyes shining, the whole face transfigured into an almost unearthly beauty. I could not realize that my dear love sat by my side after almost two years of absence.

The professor and his wife, submitting to the inevitable, greeted me pleasantly, but without demonstration; while Hester, dear child, let her heart speak.

"It's so good to be back!" she said at our second meeting. "I am more in love with my own surroundings than ever. And I've brought home such stacks of pretty things! And you really think me improved? I'm glad of that. Do you want to know what I think of you? To use an Americanism, you are positively splendid with those lovely whiskers. My dear Hal, you are quite too handsome for a clergyman; though I don't doubt you look like a saint in your robes at dear old St. John's. How I long to see you in them! To think you should have such an important charge as the old mother church! And the rectory — is that completed?"

"Quite finished," I said. "I hope it will please you. The plans I superintended myself, remembering your wishes; and it is as convenient as pretty."

"Poor mamma!" laughed Hester. "She had such high hopes for me! She counted so much on this European tour! But I would be a poor minister's wife in spite of the honors that were within my reach; and I assure you there were several," she added seriously. "However, one of them, a Russian count, had a terribly red nose, and was almost three times my age. His castle was a horrible old barn of a place, and he had six married daughters. And then there was a German baron with a square chin; but he was so dreadfully cross-eyed, that I never could look at him without laughing. And — O Harry! there was one, that had I not been very much in love, and honorable to the last degree, I might have been tempted to flirt with. I am afraid I did, just a little."

I laughed outright at her comical assumption of penitence.

"You are forgiven," I said; but a slight twinge of jealousy followed the admission.

"He wasn't *quite* as handsome as you are; but he was nice, and so attentive! I thought I had best tell you that, though I was as true as steel to you. I did perhaps allow him to think a little more of me than he should, and I was well punished for it."

"Dear heart, how?" I asked.

"By my own self-contempt when I realized what I had done. I assure you I prayed heartily for forgiveness, but prayer and penitence seldom efface results of that kind."

Here was my opportunity for confession, but my proud man's will rebelled. The conflict within made me assume a sterner demeanor than was usual with me, even when offended. But confess to a woman! never; particularly the woman who was to be my wife.

"I see what you think," she said, "and it overwhelms me with confusion. But you are my rector, and I thought the confession due to one who was to be my second self. Ought we to have secrets from each other?" she asked sweetly.

"By no means," I answered eagerly. "I would have all your love, all your heart, all your life. What became of this young man?"

"Oh! Lord Glenlynn — a beautiful name,

you observe. Well, he didn't die, that I know of. He only pulled his mustache till I thought it would come out, and with a few bitter words took his leave. I was really very sorry for the whole thing. And mamma! Heavens! how she did storm about it! She has never forgiven me."

Should I tell her of that little episode? It is not the woman only who is lost if she hesitates.

I was on the point of speaking, when a lovely child came dancing into the room. She looked like one of Correggio's angels: a sweet and sublime beauty played over her expressive face. Her every motion was grace itself.

"Come here, Marguerite," said Hester. "This is my little English cousin, Hal. She took a great fancy to us; and, as she was an orphan, her uncle consented that she should come to America. Mamma wanted some one to take my place, you know — by and by." A blush heightened the brilliant complexion. She kissed Marguerite as she led her to me.

"This gentleman is going to be your cousin, also," she said, smiling. "She is only nine years old, Hal: isn't she lovely?"

I took the little white hand in mine. Her eyes were blue, her glorious hair fell in waves of gold below her belt. In a brief time we were acquainted. She had displayed all her little treasures, — her chatelaine watch, a turquoise ring, and a locket containing her mother's hair.

"My sweet mother is in heaven," she said; "and I will show you her picture, sometime, when every thing is unpacked. Papa was a curate; are you one?"

"I am a clergyman," I said.

"I am glad of that. I used to love papa so well in his white robes! I expect he looks like that in heaven. I know *exactly* how mamma looks, because I see her very often."

I turned to Hester, who lifted her eyebrows.

"It's a little fancy she has," she said a minute after, in an aside. "It seems to make her happier, so we don't meddle with it."

"You mean you dream of mamma," I said.

"Oh, no! you mistake me if you think that," said the little one, with a wise shake of the head, and a wondrous light in the depths of her blue eyes. "I see her just as I see you. She comes in the room; and sometimes she sits down, and sometimes she stands; but she is always so happy! I used to think she was *really* dead, but I don't any more."

"What does this mean?" I asked of Hester aside. "The child is not quite right in her mind."

"Best not notice it, dear: we don't. In fact,

we knew nothing about it till we were on the ocean, when one night — a very stormy night — I heard her talking, and, on asking her who was there, was startled by the answer, —

"Only mamma!"

I knew mother was in the next stateroom, and it puzzled me till she spoke again.

"I was terribly afraid," she said, "the boat spills over so; and it seemed to me we should go down: so I prayed; and God sent mamma, who told me there was no danger. God would take us safe to America."

I assure you I felt very solemn for a moment.

"Has she gone?" I asked.

"Oh, yes! she often comes and goes that way," was her reply.

"A strange child," I said, "but exceedingly beautiful. We must try and get this fantasy out of her head."

"Maybe you can, though I doubt it," said Hester. "But I am anxious to see the rectory. Can we go now?"

"Certainly," I said: so Hester sent the child to her mother, and we were soon on the way.

CHAPTER VI.

> "And the marriage bells they merrily rang,
>   While the maiden sang, 'Heigh-ho!
> My harp so still on the willow I'll hang:
>   He should have married me — O.
> And now I must sorrow alone, alone,
> While she sits and sings by her ain hearthstone.'"

MY love was in a mood to be pleased with every thing she saw. Still, the rectory left nothing to be desired. I had studied her convenience, and followed wishes that I had treasured up when they fell like chance words from her lips.

"Papa bought me three perfect pictures," she said, when we stood in the pretty parlor. "How lovely they will look in this light! That arch, too, is exactly what I wanted; and some stamped velvet I bought in Genoa because it was awfully cheap, will be just the thing for a *portière*. You know papa insists upon furnishing, so I shall give him *carte blanche*. I think he is secretly pleased that I resisted all mamma's attempts at match-making. In his dear big heart he thinks the world of you, I know he does. Besides, I should have disappointed him if I had been fickle."

"By the way, we are not far from there," she added, as we left the rectory, and I turned the key: "won't you go with me to Miriam's? Poor cousin Miriam! it was such a sorrow to lose her father! they were all the world to each other."

I caught my breath.

"I hope you were *very* kind to Miriam," she went on, looking up the street. "Of course you were with them in all their trouble."

"I was there some of the time," I said in measured words. "But — are you really anxious to call to-day?"

"Really and truly I am," she said, and stepped firmly on towards Miriam's house. "Why — don't you want to go? Am I taking you from any work? You said you would give me to-day and"—

"Of course I am yours to command," I said, and walked on beside her. I had not seen Miriam since I had met her that last memorable time on the street, and sent her the letter. Her mother was not well, I learned; but I had not yet had the courage to call. I excused myself by thinking, that, if my services were needed, I should be sent for.

Miriam came to the door, pale and wan. The

meeting between the cousins was very touching. She hardly noticed me, and I was glad that she felt it her duty to be formal. Then Hester went up-stairs to see her aunt, whom she found worn and ill.

"How strange it all seems!" said Hester, when we were again on the sidewalk. "Miriam and auntie are both so changed! And don't you see them often? They spoke of you as if you had been a stranger. I thought I laid my commands on you to be *very* cordial," she added playfully.

"I tried to be, I assure you," was my reply.

"But there's a sort of antipathy between you, or rather towards *you*. I can see it in every thing," said Hester. "What is the matter? Auntie said she shouldn't think of sending for you if she were ever so ill; and Miriam said, sternly, 'Hush, mother!' and there the matter dropped. Are they angry with you?"

"Not that I am aware of," I said. It was not to be expected now that I should tell my little story: Miriam and her mother had put that out of the question. "Since the captain's death, Mrs. Hope has been very cool," I added, at a venture. "We can make that all right in time."

Hester seemed satisfied.

"Auntie always was a little cranky," she said,

"and Miriam has often had to apologize for her. Uncle Hope, it seems, left them almost poor; but I am certain father will do all he can for them. Now tell me about your sisters: are they all well?"

I told her of my visit home, and how Dolly wanted to keep house for me.

"And so she may: let her come, the dear little thing! How I should love her! It would do me good to see her sweet face about the house. And you know we can afford it: I have a little purse of my own."

"We will see what Dolly says," was my answer, blessing her in my thought.

"Dolly must say yes," said Hester emphatically: and how precious she seemed to me, thus taking the initiative in a matter that was very near my heart! for I felt that Dolly needed the influence of younger and merrier life than she saw at the old homestead; needed to be won from her scholarly ambition to read Hebrew and Greek, and plod through the dusty, musty old folios in my father's library. Hitherto she had lived only in the realm of the imagination; and her affection had centred itself upon her twin brother, to the exclusion of every outside friendship. One little line in one of her letters will give the reader stronger evidence of this than all I could say.

"Dearest, if there were no Christ, I should worship you."

Love was an innate quality of her being; and I longed to have her meet with some kindred nature, upon whom she could pour out the rich treasure of her innocent heart.

"We won't be selfish in our new life," said Hester, looking up sweetly.

"It is not in you to be selfish, my love," I said fervently. "How shall I tell you what a treasure you are?"

"How? — why, in any way you please: it is only the matter of when. Wait a while till the metal is tried, and we are some years older. Then you shall tell me," she said.

Time passed on. The wedding was quietly celebrated at St. John's. We were married by the rector of St. James, the reverend Archibald Lyon. Mrs. Vaughan shed real tears, — regretful ones, no doubt, — that her daughter should have thrown herself away on a poor minister; but we were happy. Hester looked radiant, and beautiful as an angel in the loveliest wedding-dress that ever came from the hands of a French artist in bridal *trousseaus;* and Dolly, in her delicate beauty, suggested an attendant seraph. My sisters were all there; and, when I faced the throng, did Hester feel my nervous start, the trembling of my arm, as my eye encountered the pale, set face of her cousin Miriam? There she sat, at the head of the family pew, all in white, not a touch of color visible except in the wild, glittering eyes that dumbly reproached me with their unutterable agony. What right had she thus to depress and haunt me? Could I help it if she had given her love unasked? How was I to know that the inevitable tendency of many women was to worship their minister in place of their God? to set him on a pinnacle so high, that the least of his smiles meant more than the most earnest protestations of other men? Believe me, a clergyman who respects his calling, and has outgrown the vanity of inexperience, never feels flattered by these undue assumptions of reverence towards himself.

If I had but told Hester all, her loving heart would not have chided me, though she might condemn my thoughtless conduct. But, once confessed, there would have been no more concealments, on that score at least.

And now I began my work in good earnest. Work it was, too, — visiting the sick; consultations with my vestry; putting my church-study in order, for I had brought the best part of my father's books to the rectory; meeting with the scarcely known members of my flock, who were as yet to me only like faces seen in dreams;

getting acquainted with the members of the choir, a quartet of exceptionally fine voices; meeting the unavoidable cases of boredom, imbecility, mendacity, and mendicancy, which in a church of that size adhere to the congregation, and, like all other calls upon time and patience, must be answered.

It was such sweet relief to go into my own home, and find Hester occupied with womanly work, but never too busy to hurry to my arms, and nestle for a glad moment in my bosom. Then came blessed peace and rest, such as I had never looked for in my wildest imaginings.

It took me weeks, nay, months, to get wonted to the new atmosphere of this beautiful home. Hester's parents had been more than liberal in fitting up each room; giving to each a character and an harmony of its own, so that there was no dreary triviality of sameness, but real picturesque treatment of furniture and belongings. Hester's good taste was responsible for most of the details, and for the beauty and symmetry of the order of arrangement. The study was a marvel of neatness and convenience. There I was wont to write my sermons, with Hester sitting at her own table opposite mine, where she wrote her letters, read or sewed, as suited her fancy. We had a cook whose skill had been tested in the professor's kitchen, and she needed no higher recommendation. Having passed with credit from under the skilled eye of Hester's mother, the daughter could safely leave all culinary matters to her judgment and economy.

My own man, Jenkins, who had graduated under my father's eye, attended to the more ordinary household duties, took care of my horse, furnace, and stable, so that to a certain extent we were quite care-free. Jenkins was tall, lean, and supple, Irish to the backbone, and in the matter of ears prodigious. These features stood guard over an enormous pair of bushy red whiskers, and full two inches from his rather flat temples. He was devoted to my interests, and seemed more like a friend than a servant.

It was an almost ideal state of existence, save those intervals where death, and all its attendant sorrows, taxed both heart and brain. Not a day passed but little Marguerite came in from school, and she often sat down to our meals with us.

"Why won't Dolly come here?" asked Hester one day, when the meat went from table seemingly as intact as when it came in. "We want somebody to help us eat, if nothing else. And she is so pretty and sweet! Besides, when you are away, she would be such company!"

"You have so many callers, dear," I said.

"Not so very. Miriam came to-day; but I couldn't prevail upon her to stay, though she wanted to look the house all over. I told her you would be so glad, — but no. She must gather up her things, and be off. She isn't a bit cousinly. Her trouble seems to have altered her. But little Dolly might be so happy here! Who was the lady that left your study this morning with a roll of music in her hand? I happened to be out picking roses in the garden when she passed."

"It must have been the new organist, a Mrs. Stanley. Tom Tracy, our tenor, has been making application for her for some months. She seems a very lady-like person, and has, of course, a history. Her husband drinks."

"I should think he would," said Hester quietly.

I looked at my wife in astonishment.

"What do you mean?" I asked.

"I mean what I say. I don't like her face: I don't think her a woman who would try to make her husband happy. I should distrust her."

"My dear!" I said, wondering if the woman's rather exceptional beauty had roused a latent jealousy. I could really think of no other reason.

"Oh, well!" and she laughed lightly: "time

will tell. If she had applied to me instead of the rector, I should have dismissed her at once."

"Not, perhaps, if you had heard her play," I made answer. "She handles the organ with the skill and taste of a master."

"That would have made no difference," said Hester, with a pertinacity that surprised me. "I judge her by her face. What kind of a man is your tenor?"

"One of my best friends, handsome, gentlemanly, and reliable. Do you remember the Mrs. and Miss Tracy I introduced you to last Sunday?"

"Ah! do I not? There was a grief in that sweet countenance, — I speak of the elder woman, — that went to my heart. The daughter is charming. Oh, yes! I remember them."

"They are Tom Tracy's wife and daughter."

"Charming people! I must know them better," said Hester. "So," she added musingly, "Mr. Tracy has long wanted this new organist. Well, I hope you will all enjoy her music: I am sure I shall not."

"You grieve me, Hester," I said.

"I see I do. You think I am suspicious or fanciful. Never mind: I've nothing more to say about it. And, as to my impressions, am I never to speak to you about them?"

"By all means!—tell me every thing," I said eagerly. "I may be guarded by them more than you think."

"Yes: I think perhaps I had better," said Hester. "Papa always trusted to my judgment. It was his habit to ask me what I thought about people who came to him for advice."

"My darling! it shall be mine," I said as we rose from table.

"Sometimes it may be of benefit," she said gently:—"there are letters! I know the postman's ring."

Jenkins came in with six or seven letters on a beaten silver card-receiver, a *souvenir* of the Continent.

I opened mine, and laid them aside, one after the other, till I came to one from Dolly. That I began to myself, but soon read aloud.

"Mr. Templeton has been so kind as to interest himself in me. He is going to give me a place as copyist in his own office. Now I will come to you gladly if you will have me. I shall be busy only six hours a day. The rest of the time I will gladly devote to Hester and you. Now, for the first time in my life, I feel really independent," etc.

Hester clapped her hands, performing sundry little antics, that in the eyes of wise people might have seemed utterly childish, and finished by taking hold of my whiskers, and kissing me on the forehead.

"Lovely! lovely!" she exclaimed. "It is the desire of my heart, and I will gladly give her a share in you. But who is Mr. Templeton, pray?"

I explained that it was my sister Belle's *fiancé*.

"And so little Miss Independence must work for a living! We'll soon wean her from that notion. She is a lily, and ought not to toil or to spin."

CHAPTER VII.

"Love, jealousy is cruel!
   I say it lying here,
I that have loved you madly
   For many and many a year."

A LETTER THAT WILL EXPLAIN ITSELF.

MY DEAR LESLIE, — I don't want to tell you, but I must. Another anonymous letter came to me last night. I read it — how could I help it? and then I took it up with the tongs, and held it over the sitting-room fire till it writhed and scorched, as my heart did while reading it. You told me to go to the rector. Alas! he is too new, and too young. What would he think of me? Yes, I burned the letter; but its contents burned themselves first into my brain, thus. Imagine the words, — coals of fire.

"*I have warned you repeatedly of Mrs. S.* [*the same Mrs. Stanley I have spoken of before*]. *You will find that T. T.* [*that's Tom Tracy, my husband*] *has at last got her a situation as organist in St. John. Did I not warn you three months ago? None so blind as those who will not see! However, you will not be blind very long.* *A True Friend.*"

Who can this be, this "true friend," who would have me distrust my husband? O Leslie! he has been very dear to me. I married him when I was only fifteen and an orphan; and he has been to me father, mother, brother, sister, husband. I cannot think wrong of him, — I will not! And yet it is a fact that the vestry have just hired and installed this Mrs. Stanley to be the organist at St. John. I cannot yet bring myself to speak of it to Tom, though I have tried several times. I am so sorry, for I know these terrible suspicions are changing my nature. Marie takes notice.

"You are not as happy as you were, dearest mamma," she said to me the other day. "Is it because of Charley?" Dear heart! I love Charley almost as much as I do her. He has grown up under my eyes, as it were, from year to year; and his love of Marie is almost idolatry. Yet, loving him as I do, I would rather see Marie dead before my eyes than dream that she could ever be forced to suffer such torments as wring my very heart with anguish. When I see the two together, I am reminded of my own engagement, and how utterly happy we both were, Tom and I! Has it come to this, — that I suspect him who has been my darling for so many years? No, no! I am deceived: I must be. Some enemy wishes to plant thorns in my heart. Rather would I die than believe this thing — oh, yes, a thousand times! and yet — why does he never mention this woman? If he would only speak her name, or speak of her, the ice would be broken. Then I could say my say, if it killed me. But he will not confide in me. It would take so few words to lift this weight from my bosom — so few!

Perhaps I could give you a pen-picture of her — the woman. Moderately tall, more than fair, dark-gray eyes, auburn hair, features perfect in every line, a bloom on her cheek, — not of nature, I think, — lips red and tempting, and a curiously caressing manner that takes with certain people, — an assumption of childlikeness. They say — oh! why do I allow myself to use the ordinary formula of gossip-mongers! — that he has been seen on the street with her, that she visits at his office, that he has aided her with his advice — with money. They say her husband is a drunkard, and treats her vilely. Is that a reason why she should covet mine? He gives her advice gratis — many lawyers do that; he lends her money — that is a common thing among friends, and for pity: *but why don't he tell me, his wife?* I would pity her too: I would give her sympathy, aid. Why should he be so deadly silent about it? I know he is naturally secretive in business matters, but this is between souls: it imbitters my life. If I had not you, true friend, to come to, I should die. God help me! what am I saying?

Our new clergyman is much appreciated. He and his wife are a lovely couple — if he is not spoiled: *can* he be spoiled? I doubt all men. His wife's name is Hester, — the name of my dead mother, my dead sister. That endeared her to me at once. She was the daughter of the professor of Hebrew at the college, and I believe we have a prize in her. I thought she seemed to read me to the innermost core of my heart. Something in the clasp of her hand sent a thrill through me. Young as she was, it seemed to me as if I could go to her for sympathy, — yes, quicker than I would dare go to my own dear husband. Oh! I picture to myself so many terrible things! Is my fancy diseased, I wonder? I see myself on my dying-bed, and Tom, stern and unmoved, standing over me, commanding me *not* to die, and yet unwilling to say the word that would raise me, though I lay in the tomb, as did Lazarus. Is it because I am exacting, jealous? I was never jealous before in all my life; and Tom has so many, many lady friends! But open friendship, ever so ardent, never troubles me: it is these strange, secret things that others see and report, and that I am forced to notice in spite of myself.

Sometimes I am tempted to follow him, but I dare not. Suppose I should meet them together: why, they might casually have fallen into each other's society; it might be the most innocent thing in the world: but what should I do? How do I know but sudden madness might take possession of me, and I disgrace myself and him? God help me! what shall I do? Every Sunday my heavy heart hangs weights upon my feet; and so I drag myself to church, either to torment myself, or sit in silent judgment on him. Can I do this much longer? No: he must have pity on me some time. He must see that I suffer, yet never asks me why. He must notice my pallor, — I that had the ruddy color of a child in cheek and lip less than a year ago. Dear friend, what do you counsel me? I have no power to bring his mind into affinity or *rapport* with my own, else I would will him, even in his sleep, to answer my soul's torment, even with doubtful words. Sometimes I think, that, as I am not well, my mind is tinged unnaturally with the morbid condition of my body; but I have been worse physically, and yet had no sorrow like this.

Write me something of comfort, for my heart lieth like lead in my bosom: I seem to be dying for one word of comfort. Presently I shall be better acquainted with our good rector's wife, Hester. I know she will help me, young as she is; but then, after all, sympathy is but sympathy. I want the truth. Farewell.

AMY ADELINE TRACY.

CHAPTER VIII.

*"Sometimes the marriage-bells are sweet,
And sometimes harsh and bitter:
Where two discordant natures meet,
They seem for burial fitter."*

DOLLY had been with us now for some months, and I was delighted to see a decided improvement in her health. Familiarity with abstruse studies and the best literature had fitted her in a peculiar degree for the work she was engaged in during four days of the week. I was not at all surprised when I learned that she was writing tales and poems for one or two of the minor magazines. To Hester it was wonderful that a young girl reared in the country should develop into a genius. To me, who had been in earlier years her teacher as well as twin soul, it seemed natural that there should be a oneness of thought and sympathy between us, and also that she should use her power in striking out into a new and delightful venture, which was to bring both money and fame.

Hester and Dolly were like sisters when together; for then Dolly's clear, rich tones rang out in sweet old-fashioned songs, or Hester played her beloved violin, or I read to them from some new book, or perhaps, after some little coaxing, Dolly gave us one of her stories, or quaint little poems, before publication.

You may fancy us seated about the great centre-table, whose wrought cover was the work of Hester's cunning fingers. Just under the gaslight sits Dolly, a picture fair to see, the rose-color of maiden modesty, as she lisps in musical numbers, or reads us a charming prose-sketch.

"Now, this, I think, should be set to music," said Hester, after Dolly had read a poem entitled, "What Was It to Me?"

She ran to the piano.

I knew this old tune would fit it, she said, laughing. "Listen!"

> If you knew what was brewing, O lady mine!
>   You wouldn't sit there so calm and sweet,
> With the golden missal upon your knee,
>   And the silken hassock under your feet.
> You'd storm and rage; and that yellow hair,
> It wouldn't be safe, perhaps, to tear.
>   But then, what is it to me?
>
> If you only knew, O lady proud!
>   That down in the primrose-covered bower,
> Your Geraldine, with her eyes so blue,
>   And her scarlet lips, and her queenly dower,

Listens to one who has never a *sou*,
And is low as the lowest peasant to you!
    But then, what is it to me?

The boy is handsome and bold and vain,
    With a pride as grand as my lady's own.
He painted the pretty Geraldine
    As a royal princess, his heart her throne;
And his love grows stronger, his hopes more wild,
Till now he is seeking to win the child.
    It may be something to me!

. . . .

My lady has risen in wrath, and thrown
    Her golden, carven missal down;
She will hie herself to the rosy bower,
    Her soul all fire, her face all flame;
She will rage like a Fury at him, I ween,
And threaten the Lady Geraldine
    With many a woe, ah me!

. . . .

And so he lingers in vain, in vain,
    For the ancient castle is empty now.
I can see him walking the oaks between,
    With no one to listen to song or vow;
For the ladies are sailing over the deep,
And I, the butler, the household keep.
    It was fifty pound to me.

"What a mercenary wretch!" said Hester as she left the piano, and resumed her knitting. The door-bell rang.

"Good-by, comfort," added my wife. "Somebody for you, no doubt. Dolly, we'll go into the other room."

"Wait a while," I said: "it may be some one to see you."

Jenkins made his appearance.

"A couple to be married, sir," he announced with due solemnity. "Will you have them in?"

"Of course I'll have them in."

"You and Dolly must remain as witnesses," I said.

"On one condition," said Hester,— "that I shall have the fee."

I readily promised her she might. I could safely do that without detriment to my exchequer. These unheralded marriages are seldom remunerative. I went into the study for my robe, and, presently coming back, found my visitors waiting. The groom was good-looking, young, tall, angular, but not ungraceful. The young lady was *petite* and very pretty; and her dress, though by no means costly, Hester afterwards assured me was a marvel of good taste.

There was something about the two that roused my curiosity. He was somewhat restless, and seemed anxious to hurry on the ceremony: she looked about in a frightened way, and did not seem at her ease until she met his kindly glance that seemed to re-assure her.

I examined the certificate. It was correct as far as I could judge, and I had proceeded half through the marriage service when the bell rang furiously.

"A mad woman, sir," said Jenkins, as a tall woman passed by him, throwing aside his outstretched arm, and rushing into the room.

Mad she certainly seemed, with eyes aflame, burning cheeks, and garments evidently thrown on in great haste.

"Sir, I forbid this marriage! I forbid it! Don't you say another word!" she gasped, as she placed herself between me and the two lovers.

"Mother! for God's sake, let us alone!" said the man in a husky voice. "Haven't you tormented us enough?"

"I say you shall never marry her, never! Sir, he is not of age;" and she turned to me, glaring.

"But his certificate says of lawful age," I ventured.

"I am: I swear it," said the young man, much excited. "My mother hates Ida: she has always hated her."

"She shall never be your wife with my consent; and, if you marry her, I will curse you!" was the savage retort.

"O Sam! I couldn't bear that," said the young girl, now speaking for the first time, her eyes full of tears. "I would be a good wife to you, Sam, indeed I would; but if I *knew* she cursed me, — your mother! — I'd never hold up my head again."

"She's got that much sense," muttered the woman.

"Mother, do you want to see me ruined for life, just to gratify your resentment?" said the young fellow pleadingly. "I promise you I'll be just as good a son, ay, and better, with Ida for my wife. You know we were children together, and I love her."

"You shall never marry that girl!" said the woman, setting her lips together.

"Mother! hear me;" and the man, white as a ghost, stretched forth pleading hands. "Mother, let me reason with you. You loved my father as I love Ida: would you have given him up at any one's bidding? I cannot give Ida up: I need not give you up because she becomes my wife. You will gain a daughter, not lose a son. O mother! be kind, be good! I have always been dutiful to you in reason: don't wreck my life! say that I may marry Ida — only say yes, mother!"

"I would rather follow you to your grave," said the relentless woman.

"Then, you shall," he said, his face taking on a stony calm as he put his hand in his breast-pocket.

"There will be murder done," said Hester, in a low voice. I put my wife and sister behind the *portière*. When I came back, the man stood in a defiant attitude, a small, gleaming revolver in his right hand. The girl, his bride to be, with moans indescribable, embraced his knees: his mother stood stern, still, but trembling like a leaf.

"Now, mother, if you don't let this marriage service go on, I'll shoot myself through the head, and you *shall* follow me to the grave," he said, in a desperate, defiant voice. "Parson, please to conclude. At the first word, remember, mother, I'll blow my brains out."

I was irresolute. What was my duty?

"If I am to proceed," I said quietly, "you must put that weapon up. This sacred service must not be made a burlesque: nor do I think a man with murder in his heart is fit to take the solemn pledges of wedlock."

"O Sam, dear! he is right. Put that terrible pistol away — put it away, dear. Perhaps it will be best."

"Perhaps what will be best?" he asked, softened by the girl's tears and sobs.

"To leave it all, just now: it would be awful to be married in this way. If your mother can't like me, we'll wait a while. I haven't any mother, and I should be so happy to have one! but — I couldn't be happy with her curse upon me."

The childish face was so grieved, so pitiful! I felt myself drawn towards her, and could not blame Sam for the stand he had taken. I could see that his mother was a little touched by the girl's tears.

"Madam," I said, turning to the older woman, "what have you against this young lady?"

"She is a foolish, ignorant girl. She couldn't make a loaf of bread to save her life. She's not the one I would have chosen for him, with a snug little home of her own, and a capable, stirring woman in the bargain."

"And twice my age, sir," said the young man, disdain in his voice, and fire in his eye. "A woman I never liked, and couldn't love if she was the only woman in the world. No, sir: I want Ida, and Ida wants me; and if she's ignorant, having been in a shop all her life, she's teachable, and sweet and affectionate:—and the amount of the matter is, sir, I love her, and she loves me."

"Are you of age?" I asked, not caring to let him know I thought his argument convincing.

"I am, sir."

"He's not, sir—within a month," said his mother sharply.

"Mother, why will you thwart me?" he turned to her pleadingly. "You know I'd obey you in any thing reasonable. You'll drive me to death's door — you've almost done it now. And Ida would make you a good daughter: she never knew a mother's love, and she can't live knowing that you hate her. Won't you try her? mother, dear, won't you?"

"I'll have nothing more to say," was her reply; "and I'll have nothing more to do with you or her. You can get along without me. What's a mother when a wife comes?" and with a cry that was partly grief, partly hate, she turned, and left the room.

"Oh, well!" the young man said, after a pause: "mother'll get over it. I'm all she's got, and it has made her selfish. I'm afraid she wouldn't want me to marry any one. But, you see, I've furnished two or three rooms nicely, and I thought perhaps mother would come and live with us. Not that she need to, for she's got a good home of her own; but it was Ida who wanted her, poor child! She didn't think, when she bought the orange-blossoms, she was going to have such a time as this. Come, Ida: parson'll finish, I reckon."

My sympathies were with the sad little woman, and so, I knew, were Hester's.

"Yes: as your mother has no valid reason to forbid the banns, I think I am authorized in completing the ceremony," I said; and with tears and blushes Ida stood up once more, and

I had almost pronounced them man and wife when Sam's mother rushed in again.

"O Sam! I can't give you up! I won't give you up! If you marry that girl, you'll sign my death-warrant. What has she done for you?— worked, starved, fought, all but died, to bring you up to respectable manhood? Has she done all that? And now you desert me for that child!"

"Mother," said Sam deprecatingly, "you're too late. Go on, sir."

I finished the ceremony. Then Sam did something that did honor to his head and heart. He left his wife. He went to his mother, put his arms about her; and as she stood there, pallid and suffering, he kissed her two or three times. The action was very fine. She melted down, too, and laid her head on his shoulder, sobbing softly.

"Now, mother, you'll love Ida, won't you?" asked Sam.

"Don't ask me," sobbed the woman. "She's got you now, and I don't feel like loving anybody."

At that moment the *portière* was rushed back; and there stood Hester, like a beneficent fairy, at the side of a table loaded with cake, fruit, and flowers.

"If she won't love you, I will," she said, caressingly, to the little, trembling bride, as she led her into the back parlor. "Come, madam, we are all going to be good friends hereafter," she added as she turned to the irate mother. "We'll have a little wedding-feast, to commemorate the occasion; and I shall take it very hard if you don't come too."

Strangely enough, in a few moments we were chatting and laughing about the improvised board; and I was blessing Hester in my heart, for I soon saw she had completely won over Sam's mother. An hour later we all sat together discussing the exciting incident. Hester was folding and unfolding a five-dollar bill.

"I'm glad it was a five," she said: "there is something uncomfortably mean in the look of a two-dollar marriage-fee."

We had hardly seated ourselves, and Dolly had the manuscript of a story in her hand, ready to read it aloud, when the bell rang again.

"It's half-past nine," said Hester, looking up at the clock. "Well, this time somebody *must* be dying! Dolly, let's go to bed."

CHAPTER IX.

"There are mysteries that we cannot fathom, even in our daily surroundings."

DOLLY gathered up her papers as we heard the shuffling footsteps of Jenkins.

"The poor fellow was getting a little nap by the kitchen-fire, I dare say," said Hester. "He walks as if he were asleep."

The door burst open, and there stood Marguerite, looking as if she rejoiced in our astonishment.

"Where, in the name of the fairies, did you come from?" ejaculated Hester.

"Home," said the girl, untying the scarlet ribbons at her chin.

"Not by yourself?"

"Oh, no! John came with me; and he smoked his pipe all the way," she added, with a look of disgust. "I smell of it, even in my bonnet-strings."

"I don't know what mother was thinking of," said Hester.

"She wasn't thinking of it anyway, I expect," said the child nonchalantly, coming towards the table, and swinging her hat as she walked. "She went up to cousin Miriam's early in the evening, and then she sent word she shouldn't be back to-night. Miriam's mother is worse, I guess."

"And what made you think of coming here, puss?" asked Hester. "Were you afraid?"

"No, indeed!" — then she went up closer to Hester. — "Mother told me I must."

"What a singular hallucination!" I said angrily. "Shall we never break the child of it?"

"Why didn't you come earlier?" queried Hester.

"I was in at Allie Campbell's" (their next-door neighbor) "all the evening, playing games. It was nine when I went home, and I was getting ready to go to bed when mother told me."

"And father was willing to let you come?" asked Hester.

"Oh! he don't care," said Marguerite. "He was busy in the library with the students' exercises, and he would have said yes to every thing."

"Oh, well! it's all right enough. She can sleep with you, Dolly;" and Hester was taking up the night-lamp when Marguerite spoke.

"Say, cousin Hester, have you got a trunk-room?"

"Why — yes," said Hester, looking up. "I suppose that's what they call it, at the top of the house."

"And is there a broken statue in it? — the Polly something — I've forgotten the name."

"What in the world do you ask me for, child?" asked Hester. "Why, yes, — didn't you have that Apollo carried up there till we could send it to be mended?" she asked, turning to me.

The question recalled to me the fact that I had sent the statue up by Jenkins, but did not know where he put it.

"It is certainly up-stairs somewhere," I made reply.

"Oh! that's where it is," said the child confidently. "Mother knows!"

I was conscious of a decidedly creepy sensation along my spine. Marguerite was manipulating the *papier-maché* cutter that I had been using.

"Well, and suppose it is: what of it?" asked Hester, still lingering.

"I'll tell you what *she* said," was Marguerite's reply: "'If you will go up into cousin Hester's trunk-room, with cousin Hester and cousin Hal, they shall hear me talk to you.'"

"Gracious heavens!" cried Hester, turning

to me: "did ever you hear such a monstrous proposal?"

"And then," continued the child, turning over the pages of a magazine, "she said the trunk-room was up-stairs under the roof, with the broken statue of Apol — Apol" —

"Apollo Belvedere," said Dolly.

"Hal, suppose we go up there, just to see," said Hester. "I don't know where the statue is, neither do you: come, dear, just to please me. It would be curious enough if she should know what neither of us do."

"Nonsense! there's no *she* about it, and you know it," I muttered; but nevertheless I was a trifle curious; and Hester and I went upstairs, unconscious that Marguerite followed us stealthily.

Arrived at the trunk-room, sure enough there stood the statue, the broken arm lying on the floor.

"I told you she said so!" said Marguerite, startling me so suddenly that I seemed to lose my strength, and was for leaving the room; but Hester's hand was on my arm.

"Now we are here, dear," she said softly, "I should like to try — to see, that is — if — we could hear any thing, you know."

"I'll not have to do with the works of darkness," I said, backing to the door.

"But, Hal, just to please me, dear," said Hester. "I have a great curiosity — I always have had — to see something of that kind; and, if I could judge for myself, it would be so much pleasanter! It certainly can do us no harm."

"But what would be said, Hester? I, a minister of the gospel! I can't sink my profession"—

"Nobody need ever know it," said Hester; "and *we* sha'n't hear any thing. I've no faith, you know — only I should like — to try."

"Well, what have we to do? Of course there's nothing in it; but just to please you, as Marguerite is here."

"Yes, yes: what are we to do?"

"What are we to do, Marguerite?" I asked.

"Nothing," came in a low voice: "she is here now. I see her."

"Hester, go down: this is unhallowed," I said. And then I think I felt the hair rise on my temples; for a low voice, almost a whisper, distinctly said, —

"And he that was dead came forth."

"Marguerite," said Hester.

"Yes," was the quiet reply.

"Was it you who spoke just now?"

"Oh, no, indeed!" was the earnest, calm reply: "it was mother."

"Angels and ministers of grace defend us!"

I exclaimed. "Let us get out of this. I don't know whether the ground is holy or unholy, but let us get out."

Hester opened the door.

"I shouldn't like to hear it again," she said, trembling.

"It was Marguerite," I said.

"Oh, no, no! don't let the child hear you: it would grieve her terribly."

"Of course she was unconscious, but it was she."

We went down-stairs, leaving Marguerite at Dolly's door; and the child went in.

Every thing in the pleasant parlor looked unreal. Had I, or had I not, heard a voice from the dead?

Hester and I talked it over: it was so out of the order of things that Marguerite should have come over at that hour, and, altogether, the child was unique. I couldn't make it out, though I puzzled my brains till midnight. Evidently I had been deceived: perhaps my own ears had deceived me. But Hester had heard it as plainly as I had, and she was very pale while we talked it over.

"It's all very well," she said, "now we have heard it, but I don't want to hear it again. What a strange child Marguerite is! She's not in any way different from other children in her manners, just as childish — only in that strange gift. Oh! but, Hal, some way it convinces me that there is truly a life beyond the grave."

"You don't tell me that you ever had any doubts!" I said, rather startled.

"I don't know — I'm afraid that sometimes — O Hal! I am so afraid of dying, and leaving you! oh, so afraid! It don't seem as if any beyond could compensate me: it don't seem as if there could be any beyond!"

She hid her face on my shoulder.

"Not that I don't try to be a good Christian," she said a moment after, with tearful eyes and quivering lips; "but naturally I doubt every thing. Papa used to say that I saw things too quickly — that I didn't reason enough; and I suppose I don't. Sometimes when you preach such glowing sermons of the heavenly beyond, I am lifted up, even to the pearly gates: but when your voice is still, when I see all the commonplace people steeped in their commonplace duties, and never seeming to look beyond themselves, then that cold shiver of doubt comes over me; and — I'm glad of what I heard to-night, though I can't realize, and can't believe it. Now, father-priest, I have made my confession, and you must deal with me. What sort of a penance must I perform?"

"Love me dearly, and leave your future with

God. You need not fear, dear wife, while your life is so full of kindly offices for others and for *Him*."

"I hope He will spare us for a long life of usefulness, and then take us together," she said, to which I echoed a hearty Amen.

In the morning Marguerite took breakfast with us, chatting like a magpie, utterly forgetful, apparently, of the singular occurrence of the past night. To me it all seemed like a dream. I did not credit my own senses, and tried to dismiss the matter from my mind. All this was as nothing, however, compared with what came afterwards, in the shape of a note from Marguerite.

"DEAR COUSIN HESTER, — You know I went from your house to school, thinking there was no need to go home. Well, I got all my lessons to perfection, and went home early. Mrs. Moss met me at the door, holding up both hands.

"'To think what you've been saved from, child!' she said.. 'It's a meracle.' Then she took me up-stairs into my own little room, and there was my bed crushed and broken by the ceiling which had fallen on it in great masses. I should have been killed, so that's why mamma sent me to you. Isn't God good?"

Mrs. Moss was the housekeeper.

Hester read the little missive, and the tears welled up to her eyes.

"It does seem as if she had a special protector," she said.

"We all have," said Dolly; "but this certainly was providential in a wonderful degree."

That afternoon Hester's mother called; and I was behind the *portière*, filling out a marriage certificate. Hester pulled up the big chair, and saw her mother settled comfortably, and then they talked of ordinary matters till Hester spoke of Marguerite.

"So queer of the child to take a notion to come here that hour of the night, wasn't it? Well, it saved her life; and I've been talking to father about that ceiling for months. Now we've got to have it in new; and I'm determined to turn the room into a library, and have a handsome ceiling, now we're about it. It will all have to be done up, and there's a room just as good for Maggy."

"How is aunt Hope?" asked Hester.

"Better to-day — had one of her sinking-spells yesterday, and I really think she'll go if she has another. She don't seem to realize how ill she is, — ill sounds so much better than sick, you know: we learned that in England, and very glad am I that we did."

"Don't Miriam leave the house, ever?" asked Hester. "I don't know when she has been here."

I could see Mrs. Vaughan at this question open and shut her reticule, shake her head, purse up her lips, and look very prim and grim. She had heard of that little episode, and had once essayed to lecture me; but I had cut her short with rather unclerical acerbity, and she had not forgotten it.

"Miriam, poor child! has had her troubles too. No, she seldom goes out. She is a most devoted child. I'm afraid she is working beyond her strength."

"Of course she is devoted," says Hester: "she ought to be. It's her own mother she's caring for. Only it would be better for both if Miriam would take more exercise. I think she might come and see us once in a while."

"She *might* come to see *you*," says Mrs. Vaughan, with impressive emphasis. I see the solemn shake of the head, the tightly shut lips.

"And, pray, why not *us?*" asks Hester, her voice a trifle sharper.

"Oh! I dare say she has her reasons," is the evasive reply.

"I dare say she has," says Hester; "but I do think she might be more cousinly. I always liked Miriam, but she doesn't seem to like me. Well, she must judge for herself."

"We don't know everybody's private experience," says Mrs. Vaughan significantly.

"It's well we don't," Hester responds.

"Yes, perhaps — only don't judge Miriam harshly, poor child! She makes no *confidantes*, but I can tell you she has been sadly deceived."

"For patience' sake!" cries Hester: " I never dreamed that of Miriam. Who was it? I didn't know she ever had a lover except that bald-headed Pinkerton. You don't tell me that he blighted her young affections! Miriam never seemed to me to care to be settled in life. Who was the blighter? Please tell me. Was it while I was away?"

At this stage of the conversation I see fit to raise the curtain, and make my appearance on the carpet. Of course Miriam's name is dropped — for this day only.

CHAPTER X.

"No sense, no wit, no humor, only a figure-head, a woman lacking in all things but vanity."

MIRIAM! Why should the mere mention of her annoy me? I had put her out of my life so completely, that, unless her name was brought up in some such way as Mrs. Vaughan had mentioned it, it never occurred to me. The Hopes had long ago given up their pew. Miriam never came to church. When she called, which, as Hester had said, was but seldom, she never remained till I came in the house; and of late Hester seldom spoke of her.

As soon as my wife's mother left us, I went into the study. It was quite dark. The gas burned low. I turned it up, and was about to sit down, when the notion took me to go into the chancel. I knew the choir had stopped practice, and had probably gone. It therefore surprised me somewhat to hear voices as I stood there quite hidden by the darkness. There was only one light burning in the choir; and by it I saw the face of my tenor, Tom Tracy. He had an exceptionally fine, pure face. I had often wondered why a man who had so little sympathy for the offices of religion could so carry the countenance of a saint. But Tom was not alone. Now and again I heard a low, musical laugh, and then a woman's voice, subdued but ringing.

"O Tom! as if I could forget."

Turning uneasily, I met Jenkins's inquisitive orbs fastened on my face. There was a keen intelligence in his glance.

"Do they often stop in this way, Jenkins?" I asked.

"As a gineral thing," said Jenkins, still eying me. His ears seemed fairly to vibrate with intelligence.

The words that my wife had spoken forced themselves upon my memory, —

"I don't like her face. I don't think her a woman who would try to make her husband happy."

Then the countenance of Mrs. Tracy came before me, — the look of habitual grief, the effort of her smile, the something unexplainable by which the least practised eye can read the secret of a heart wounded to the core. A quick tremor ran through my veins as though the matter were personal to myself; and I hurried back into the study, angry with Tom Tracy, and disgusted with the organist for daring to use his name so familiarly.

Another mood took me. I went in the chancel, and walked down the aisle, humming audibly. The clock said half-past eight: my eyes were steadfastly fixed on the dial. The talk ceased; and Tom came down the choir-steps with a smile as serene as that of an angel, followed by Mrs. Stanley, upon whose fair, false face the light was strongly reflected as she passed me. A large broad-brimmed hat shaded her great, passionate eyes; and her hair, partly curled, lay in masses on her forehead. That she was beautiful, as men count beauty, could not be denied.

"We got through earlier than usual," said Tom, with the frankness of a child. "I think we'll try Steiner's *Te Deum* next Sunday for the first time."

"Very well," I answered in a constrained voice. "How is your wife, Mr. Tracy?"

"Well, thanks, she is about as usual, — complaining a little; never quite on the rugged order; constitutional sort of thing," he answered cherubically.

He passed out of the church-door after a commonplace sentence or two, and walked down the yard with Mrs. Stanley, she with her arm in his. What right had I to watch them, with an almost irresistible desire to tear them asunder? I was no knight-errant to fight for other men's wives; so I bottled up my wrath, and entered my study again.

Behold, it was tenanted! A woman, her tangled hair escaping from a nondescript bonnet, her hands half gloved, the wrinkled backs coming just over her coarse red knuckles, sat in my study-chair, apparently reading the open letter that lay on my desk.

"Oh, dear! I do beg your parding"—and here she pulled out a hair-pin, and thrust it, with a bunch of frowsy hair, on the other side of her forehead. "I had so little time along of the baby's bein' sick (he's my sevingth, and his name is George Chartres Magnolia Dickory), that, says I to Mr. Dickory (a tailor, sir, and fitting with that accuracy that you'd declare the clothes was pasted on. In Hingland it was he learned his trade: he and me be both Hinglish born),—and says I to him at supper, 'I have not treated the new minister with proper respect. Halpin (which is his first name, and named after the second cousin of his father, which were a clergyman of the Church of Hingland) and you must wash the dishes, and tend to the children, particularly giving George Chartres his drops every ten minutes.' You see, it is so hard for me to git out of the house, doin' my own work as I does, — no housekeeper, no nurse, no cook, as my mother had before me, — that I have to neglect many of my social duties. Well, and how are you? and how do you like us here?"

Taken aback at this flow of words, at the remarkable appearance of my unlooked-for visitor, in whose face was a mingling of shrewdness, good nature, and vulgarity, and in her manner an audacity which was not the result of ignorance mainly, but of an intense self-esteem, I could not have spoken but for the time she gave me to collect my thoughts.

The name seemed familiar to me, but I had forgotten in what connection I had heard it spoken of; and it only haunted me as the echo haunts the voice, with no definite result.

"I thank you," I made reply, seating myself on the lounge, leaving her master of my desk and of me: "I am pleased with the people, and very comfortable at present."

"Indeed, I am glad to hear that;" and she made a futile effort to draw her gloves over her bony hands. "I spoze maybe you didn't know dear old Mr. Stillwater, as was the last rector. We fairly idolized him; and I was that familiar in the family, that I'd go in without knocking. He baptized all my dear children, savin' and accepting George Chartres Magnolia, which I hope to have the pleasure of seeing him crossed under your hands, trusting your benediction will make a man of him. And his coats always did fit without no effort on his part. He just put himself in the hands of Mr. Dickory without reserve; and if they was ordered at nine at night, to be done at four in the morning, Dickory was the man to be on time if he had to set up two nights to do it. Its a hard-working parish, too; and it takes all one's time to go over it, as I know who always carries my husband's work home; and plenty of custom he have, always willing to take care of the children: and turn and turn about is my motto for married folks. To be sure, house-work doesn't come so handy to the men, especially if they haven't been brought up to it; but they do very well if they practise, as they all ought to. It's their privileges, only they don't know it. But la! you haven't been married long enough to know: wait till you git a houseful of children yourself."

By this time I was utterly disgusted. I had never met in all my life, ministerial or otherwise, a character so offensive; and it made me tremble for my own manhood. I felt an almost irresistible desire to rise up, and order her to the door, more than once, or to give her a piece of my mind. Come what would, she should never have the opportunity to trouble Hester, or any of my household. I do not think I have in any case a large share of grace: the human is constantly knocking at the door of the spiritual, and demanding entrance, with all its faults and foibles, its little weaknesses and tempers. I saw in my mind's eye the copious possibilities of future annoyance, both to my wife and myself, in this very respectable but voluble and unpleasant person, and mentally decided to encourage neither her nor her husband. How many more of these purely material natures, as opposed to the ideal characters I had mentally assigned to the different portions of the congregation, I had under my spiritual care, I had yet to learn. This evening's experience had unfolded two extremes in the persons of Mr. Tom Tracy and Mrs. Dickory. One of my friends had warned me against several whom he denominated cranks, among them several noted for miserly qualities, and others for unbridled temper, the latter usually stirring the parish to a ferment once or twice a year.

"Well, I must go," said Mrs. Dickory, graciously vacating the rector's chair, and pulling her gloves half way over her knuckles in a vain effort to make them smooth. "I *should* like to have seen your wife; though I really did expect, from what I heard, that her cousin would step into her shoes, as the sayin' is. I shall be sure to come to church as often as I can, though I must always bring the children."

"All of them?" I was surprised into saying.

"Oh, no! Dickory will take care of the babies:" and, with the oddest series of bows and nods it was ever my experience to behold, she took her leave; and I sat listening to her departing footsteps.

"Well!"

It was an ejaculation that had meaning. I looked up. There stood Hester, her beautiful face cameo-like, brilliant against the background of the darkness.

"Have they all gone?" she asked.

"The choir? oh, yes! long ago."

"I am so disappointed! I even sent Dolly into the study for you, but you were nowhere to be seen. We have had visitors — such visitors!"

"And I have had *a* visitor! such a visitor!"

"Who was it, pray?"

"Mrs. Dickory."

"What! is her husband a tailor?"

"So she says."

"O Hal! she will kill you!" and Hester laughed. "You have passed your examination with credit, I hope. Have either of the young

Dickories chicken-pox or measles? I assure you, she would come to you sooner than to the doctor. O Hal! I pity, but I cannot help you; for, if she ever comes to me, I shall snub her. But there's this consolation, — if the act on my part is uncharitable or unchristian, she won't know it. You haven't asked yet who *our* visitors were."

My darling had by this time ensconced herself in the rector's chair; and this picture so effectually effaced the other, that I was myself again, and of course asked the expected question.

"Well, do you know Mrs. Whitby of the Elms? Yes, of course you do. It was she who came, bringing with her a live count! — a fragment of the old French nobility, though he walks through this weary world as plain Mr. Ravaillac. But, my dear, he is the most distinguished-looking man I have met out of his native element, the air of France. I do assure you he is charmingly handsome, and accentuates his language delightfully."

"You are certainly enthusiastic over a stranger," I said, a little nettled.

"No more than you will be when you see him," said Hester. "Just ask Dolly! I introduced her as Mary, and it was delicious to hear him pronounce it as Marie. Haven't you written your sermon yet? Oh, pray let me finish it!"

"I beg you to do so," I said.

I had left the last sentence thus:—

"Finally, beloved"—

"Shall I add, 'disciples of the proper?'" she asked, and then wrote on,—

"Finally, beloved, go home in peace, eat your dinners in amity, scold your wives in leniency, punish your children in equity, sand your sugar in scarcity, water your milk in paucity, speak of all men (and women too) in charity, live as you should in purity, and I promise you as a surety you will go to the regions of the honest and the try-to-do-right in the sublime radiance of the great hereafter."

I did not see what she had written till the following day, when I had forgotten the circumstance. She had spoiled a sheet of my sermon paper; but I followed out her suggestions, after a hearty laugh all to myself, which brought Jenkins to the door, with his long ears as red as beets, and his blue eyes protruding like saucers.

"Never mind, Jenkins," I said: "it was something I was thinking of."

CHAPTER XI.

"One cannot tell what virtues he possesses, but he speaks three languages."

ON the following Sunday, Mrs. Whitby, who occupied the third pew from the chancel, came to church, accompanied by her eldest daughter Mabel and the French count. Mrs. Whitby was rich, handsome, stylish, capable, and — Mrs. Whitby of the Elms! She lived in a palace of a house, whose adornments my poor pen could but faintly portray. Mr. Whitby was a merchant, and one of the few rich men of my parish, bald-headed, red-faced, and pompous. He cared little for splendor, and all for business. His stores took up whole blocks; his ships navigated every ocean; his schemes were stupendous, and never failed. He had clerks by the score: and one of the best of these was Monsieur Ravaillac, who, on account of his ability to translate in three different languages, received a much larger salary than his fellows; and on account of his misfortune in having been reduced from the ranks of the nobility to the ranks of the *canaille*, poor fellow! had the *entrée* of the Elms, and was a privileged character at all their entertainments.

If you ever met a man with a Greek face, English shoulders, and a French mustache, you have seen Ravaillac's double, perhaps. I did not wonder at my wife's enthusiastic description of the fellow. He was handsome enough to warm the heart of a statue. Only a few weeks passed before he became a constant caller at our house. His varied accomplishments — musical, literary, and æsthetic — made him a more than agreeable companion. He spoke English intrepidly, with now and then a lapse that made his sentences inimitable, and so impressed one, that to forget them was impossible. The Greek beauty of his face was of the most commanding type. I soon saw, what became apparent to every one, that Dolly was the magnet that attracted him. Add to a magnetic countenance a mind of exceptional strength, the utmost refinement in manners, and a spirit apparently thoroughly imbued with high principles and religious sentiments, and what young girl would not feel flattered by the attentions of such a man?

My wife was delighted.

"As sure as you live, he'll marry Dolly," she

said one evening when we were talking it over, "and take her to Paris. It is just delightful to hear him talk of his home in Paris; his little grandmother, whose devotion to the Bonapartes is still undiminished; and his lovely sister Elise, who is married to a colonel in the French army. He is a scion of the old nobility, too; and I declare, I have a reverence for old families, myself; and I believe everybody has. He will bring the picture of his sister, whom he speaks of as *mon ange*, to-night. It is very sweet to hear the tender expressions that fall from his lips when he refers to her. Mrs. Whitby says he is very popular among her acquaintances; and don't you think him fond of Dolly?"

"I have noticed it," I said, as she brought round the silken cord of the dressing-gown she had just helped me into.

"Yes, of course you have. It is dear little Dolly's greatest ambition, you know, to travel. How much it would add to her varied accomplishments! I wish she could have gone in my place: I never really cared so much about it. But Mr. Ravaillac is such a gentleman! there's only—only"—she hesitated; then, as her eyes caught mine, she laughed.

"Only a tiny bit of a doubt, hardly born yet, that he may not be *quite* what he assumes; but it only comes to me now and then, and is not big enough to stand alone. It makes me rather watchful, that's all, for Dolly's sake, you know. Oh! by the way, I am going to call on that pretty Mrs. Tracy to-day, your tenor's wife; and I shall also take in the Hopes on my way home. I'm afraid aunt Hope is very ill. Papa was there yesterday."

That night Hester, as was her usual habit, recounted the incidents of the day.

"And did Mrs. Tracy confirm your previous impressions?" I asked.

"More than that," she said. "She gave me the first genuine heart-ache I ever had in my life."

"She was very unhappy, then?"

"On the contrary, brilliant, and seemingly overflowing with life. Her house and its appointments, but for her exquisite taste, would be like a bazaar of Oriental splendor. But, oh, dear! she is not happy."

"And yet you intimate that she was gay."

"Apparently. But once I touched a secret spring, that shadowed the beauty both of house and hostess. On a bracket stood an exquisite medallion,—a face painted in oils. I exclaimed admiringly, but it was the painter's art that surprised me. I had quite forgotten the face, and yet it seemed to me that I had seen it before.

"'Do you like it?' she asked; and a strange intensity changed her voice.

"'No — I don't like it — exactly,' I made reply: 'there is something false in the face.'

"Then it flashed over me who it was; for I saw her cheek pale, and her lip quiver.

"'She is a friend for whom my husband procured a situation,' she said.

"'And she sent that as a token of her gratitude?' I asked, astounded.

"'Oh, no! my husband bought that of the artist who painted it. I think it was her brother, and he was in great need.'"

"I see no real harm in that," I said.

"Don't you? well, I do;" and my Hester's gentle eyes flashed. "Why didn't he order some other picture? To set that up before the eyes of his wife! I'd have thrown it into the fire! Better to die than be so insulted! There are things that men have done, honorable men so called, that they have never told their wives. Perhaps, the temptation having passed, and the deeds been repented of, that is best; but it is well *you* had nothing to conceal."

She took my hand caressingly.

"And that is why I felt my happiness would be safe in your keeping, for I have a tendency to be desperately jealous — but only for cause, sir," she added, smiling. "I knew a clergyman, as a mere man, was no better than others; but, as a priest, his calling imposed upon him the strictest watch over his own inclinations, and the most guarded care over his own nature, that he might be a guide to others."

"And was this all of your interview with Mrs. Tracy?" I asked, feeling a certain little stab as she thus unconsciously arraigned me before the tribunal of my own conscience.

"Oh, dear, no! I found out that she was the most wretched woman, with her affectation of light-heartedness, that I ever met. Her daughter came in from a neighbor's while I was there, — a delicate, lovely creature, with an aureole of true golden hair, and the blue of her eyes was as blue as heaven. By the way, she watched her mother, hung on her words, touched her with such soft touches, — every movement a caress. I could see that she, too, suffered. Oh, some day I shall hear such a story! I am sure of it, and it will make me miserable."

"No: you shall not take upon yourself the sorrows of my parishioners," I said. "That is my duty and my cross."

"And I am not to help my husband in the sterner calling of his pastorate? Did you choose me only to set me over your household gods, to pet you when you are tired, and to watch you doing good afar off? No, no: I am better than that, woman though I am. I love home dearly, but I want to feel that I am a helper as well as a comforter outside of home."

"Did you go to your cousin's?" I asked, after giving her a kiss; for I could not gainsay her sweet fervor, though I determined she should know as little as possible of my harsh conflict with the outer world.

"Yes, and found aunt Hope very low: indeed, I knew it before. I don't believe she will live long, for Marguerite dreamed she died; and what that child dreams always comes true."

"You put too much faith in that little chit," was my rejoinder. Marguerite was not a favorite with me, on a more intimate acquaintance. There was something uncanny about the child; and I hated the mysterious, save and excepting the mysteries of our holy religion. Marguerite went to school now, a select school, two or three miles out of the city; and we rarely saw her except under the professor's roof.

"One can't ignore one's experience," said Hester. "I never told you, but one day Marguerite came over here, and said she dreamed Dick fell off his perch, dead; and the child had hardly left the house before the dear little fellow was dead. If one can't understand, one must believe. You can't ignore simple facts."

"Merely a coincidence," was my answer.

"What will your cousin do if her mother should die?"

"I think she will go home to mother's. Mother has talked it over a good deal, and is not satisfied with the school where Marguerite goes. She wants to send her to the sisters', but papa absolutely forbids that. Miriam is highly educated, you know, and could teach Marguerite at home. That would suit on all sides."

"Yes, I should think so," I said dubiously. It was not pleasant to think of Miriam as so near a neighbor. Indeed, if I could have ignored her utterly, I should have been more than glad to do so.

"It's one of the inexplicable things," said Hester, "that my aunt has taken such a dislike to you. It must be the disease affects her mind. Why, she used to call you 'that divine young man,' and was always sounding your praises before we left for Europe. It is certainly unaccountable."

"Sick people often take such freaks," I said, and changed the subject.

CHAPTER XII.

*"Sleek and fair-faced,
Assuming respectability, full of old anecdotes."*

"A GENTLEMAN to see you," said Jenkins one morning.

Jenkins stood like a great blur in the doorway; for it was blue Monday, and I was a little out of sorts. His ears looked broader and longer than ever.

"I did hope I could have an hour to myself," I said impatiently, glancing up from my paper. "Does he look like a man who needs me?"

"I can answer your question," said Hester; "for I happened to be in the study, hunting a book, when he came in. I am sure he don't want to be buried: he might possibly have a wedding in contemplation, but I shouldn't care to be the bride. Candidly, though, he is excellently well dressed, if that will help you."

"Tell him I'll be in," I said; and Jenkins disappeared.

"Seems to me," I growled, as I drew off my

dressing-gown, "that fellow's ears grow longer and larger every day."

"They couldn't very well grow smaller," said Hester. "I have often wished, myself, they could be cut down."

The notion tickled me, and I went smilingly into the study to meet an utter stranger.

"Rev. Mr. Clements," he said glibly — "delighted to see you, I'm sure. Of course you don't know who I am. I should have given your servant my card. Pangrist, my name is, — the grandson of old General Pangrist, son of Doctor Pangrist, both of them members of old St. John's: you'll find their names on your book. I came, sir, for the sake of old associations. When a child, sir, from that to a boy at college, I had the privilege of attending the dear old church. Circumstances took me away to the West, where my father emigrated when I was seventeen. I am now renewing old impressions, sir; and I say again, I am delighted to meet you."

It seemed to me I had seen the name of Pangrist, as, indeed, I had, on the church-books, only a week before. The man was so hearty in his manner, so well, nay, elegantly dressed, that he made an impression for good. I forgot that it was blue Monday, and was glad to meet an agreeable and intelligent companion. Every thing about him suggested refinement and culture. The more I talked with him, the better pleased I was. We discussed several questions on debatable matters, and he seemed at once fearless and honest in all his opinions, and sound in church-views. He spoke of several persons I knew, and seemed to have an intimate acquaintance with the various rectors.

"I would like," said he, with a childlike smile, "to look at the old church if you do not object. I really feel as if it would renew my youth to see the dear old pew where, with my sainted mother, I sat sabbath after sabbath, not exactly a willing listener, but happy wherever she was. Ah! she has long been in the church above. Have I your permission, sir?"

"Indeed," I responded with alacrity, "I shall be most happy to accompany you;" and in another moment we stood in the chancel.

"Ah! the same dear old place! no improvements," he said, as he stood there holding his hat in one hand, and gently smoothing his long black mustache with the other.

I ventured to say that the chancel had a new window.

"Ah! pardon me. I didn't observe that, but I do now. Very fine in its coloring too; rich, very rich, and the design remarkably beautiful."

"Yes: it is a memorial window, given by the widow of old Colonel Winslow."

"Ah, yes! I remember him — the venerable old man! Did you ever meet with him?"

"It was before my time," I made reply, "but I know his widow: she is very old."

"Yes: I knew her also. He was a remarkably fine specimen of the old aristocracy. And he was a gentleman, sir, an old-time gentleman, — hair white as the driven snow, urbane, courtly. We don't see many of those fine old gentlemen in these days, when so many devices are resorted to in vain attempts to restore what never returns, one's lost youth."

We walked slowly up the aisle.

"How every thing comes back to me!" said my companion with a sigh. "It is strange how, in such a place as this, the yearnings of the soul master one. The truths which are common to belief seem so much more sacred! Ah, sir! the teachings by a mother's knee are never forgotten."

"Never!" I responded fervently, feeling more and more sympathy with my new friend.

"Yes, sir: we must not be exclusive and selfish in matters of faith, and that is why I rest implicitly in the doctrines of the Church — the dear old mother! Her mission is to regenerate mankind: I feel it, sir. The time cannot be far off when the whole pagan world will come under her influence, and we shall all be the sheep of her fold.

"Here is where I sat beside my sainted mother," he said, stopping short at a handsomely decorated pew, about midway of the aisle. "Over there the Paisleys sat: I wonder if any of the family are living. Just in front of us Dr. George Littlefield and his family, — five pretty girls, sir;" and he turned to me smiling roguishly. "I leave you to decide, sir, whether a young fellow of sixteen can pay over-much attention to a sermon in view of five pretty girls, any one of them bewitching enough to turn the brain of an anchorite, let alone a poor boy who worshipped beauty.

"How it all comes back to me! the Penns, the Coles, the Mackeys, the Jedsons, the Scholleys, the Pinkertons — ah! I knew them all, sir. Excuse me, sir;" and he took out a fine white handkerchief, and pressed it to his eyes. I declare, the effect was very fine — there in the mellow light of the old church. I felt like shedding a tear or two myself.

Then he examined the various hymn-books, turned to the initial pages, and read the names.

"Alas! many of them new to me, sir; though I remember the Eddys and the Oldfields. George Oldfield was a very elegant man: it was once thought he would be the President of the United States. The Eddys drove up in their carriage and pair: it was said his horses cost him a round five thousand. He had his own sailing-vessel, too, and usually spent his summers on board. I don't know of a family with more leisure and money at their command. I wonder," he mused thoughtfully, "if his descendants have gone through the fortune, or are they rich now."

"I believe the Eddys are rich," I said; "but I think circumstances will warrant me in saying that they use their privileges very badly. In other words, this Eddy and his wife are extremely niggardly, and, when they do come to church, wear neither decent nor comfortable clothing. They have only one daughter, who by all accounts is both crippled and silly; and a boy who is deformed."

"Dear me! what degeneration! It often happens so," he said with a sigh. "The fine brain rarely transmits its superior attributes to its successor; the godly grandfather looks with sorrow on his unprincipled grandson: we cannot account for it, the wisest of us. Dear me! I never noticed till this moment — you have a modern church-organ! The one I remember was a nondescript thing, with mock brasses, and a most unearthly wheeze; while the boy invariably went to sleep over the bellows."

His description made me laugh, it was so true to the life: I remembered the old organ. The new one was put in the second Sunday of my ministration.

"It is a very fine organ, and I am proud of it," I said.

He turned to me.

"Perhaps you play," he said.

"I play after my fashion," was my reply.

"The distinctive feature of music lies in the feeling we have as performer or as hearer. I am sure you are fond of music: permit me to be a listener, if for only a few minutes."

My vanity responded. I soon had the instrument unlocked, and the bellows in full play.

"If you will pardon me," said my new friend, "I will go to the front of the chancel. There, as in viewing masses of positive color, you had best look from a given point; so, in music, I am more impressed at a little distance from the performer."

"Certainly," I said, flattered by his deferential manner, and some strong words of praise he added.

He went down towards the chancel, and I poured my soul into the music. I have the gift of improvisation, my friends are pleased to say, in a remarkable degree; and the utter silence of my hearer delighted me. After the lapse of a considerable time, I finished, and turned round. There stood my visitor like one entranced, in front of the chancel, his face alight with pleasure.

"Don't, don't stop!" he said, with an impressive movement of his hand: "it is heavenly."

But I had spent my enthusiasm, and walked towards him. We talked a little further on unimportant subjects, and then he rose to go.

"You will stay to dinner," I said. "I am sure Mrs. Clements will second my invitation."

"Thanks, thanks," he replied; "but I believe I have two other engagements, which call for all my spare time to-day. I have absolutely lengthened a call, that should have occupied minutes only, to nearly an hour. Pray forgive me, and allow me to express my sincere pleasure that the old church has so popular a rector. Oh! by the way, I am recently, as I told you before, from one of the beautiful isles of the sea; and during my travels I gathered a large collection of macaws, birds of splendid plumage, that can be trained to speech. The birds are very young; but all the better, you know, for that. Allow me to present your lady one, with my best wishes."

"Indeed," I said, "I cannot permit that. I know the birds are valuable, and you really must let me pay for it. I am sure it must have cost you to transport them to this country."

"Oh, yes! a trifle: but I could not think of taking any thing. It is a present out of respect for the dear old church. You are aware, I suppose, that they need a particular kind of cage. These are to be bought at Restwick's, New York; and, if you will write them, you can easily get one sent you. By the way, I will call there. Restwick is a friend of mine; I have bought several cages of him: and you may rely upon it, I will, by giving my personal attention, secure you a perfect one in every respect."

"Perhaps you would oblige me by paying for it, and sending it to my address, yourself," I said.

"Well — if you feel particular. I suppose it would come here much sooner. The price is only ten dollars, express-charges included. I often take little commissions from my friends."

I found a ten-dollar bill in my pocket, and put it into his hands. He gave me a receipt, and then took his leave. I felt as if parting from a valued friend.

"My dear Hal!" Hester greeted me: "why didn't you stay all day?"

I gave her certain reasons, carefully concealing the matter of the gift, and regretting that my new-found acquaintance would not stay to dinner.

"I'm so glad!" she said, drawing a long breath. I looked at her in surprise.

"Then, you didn't like him!" I exclaimed.

"There was a way he glanced round the study that I didn't like," said Hester: "it was mousey, and his eye was bad."

I sat back and laughed, but not without some inward misgivings. However, I finished my dinner, enjoyed a quiet afternoon, and next morning sent Jenkins, according to agreement, to the pier of a certain steamship company, for the bird, which was to be delivered in a small wooden cage.

Ten o'clock came, and so did Jenkins, grinning from ear to ear.

"What makes you look so pleased?" said Hester, as the man presented himself.

I winked at Jenkins, I hemmed, I scuffled my foot; but the impenetrable rascal stood there, still grinning.

"Why, there war no less than twenty gentlemen's servants, and lots of ministers, on the wharf, all waiting for birds."

"For birds!" said Hester wonderingly.

"Let me explain, wife," I began.

"And, begorra, they'll have to stand till the ind of the worrld," Jenkins went on, "before they'll git 'em! It's a swindle, sir; and they'd all paid for cages too:" and then, unrestrained by the fear of ministerial dignity, he burst into a loud guffaw.

"For pity's sake, Hal, what does it all mean?" asked Hester, as he slunk out of the door; and then I had to tell her.

"If you had only spoken to me!" she said, and then laughed till her eyes were dropping tears.

"It is too good! I shall have to tell papa. Why *couldn't* you see through him? It seems to me I could. I told you he was mousey." Suddenly she paused with a blank face.

"I left my watch and chain there," she gasped, "on your study-table — the one papa gave me, with brother Willy's hair braided in the back. O Hal! I have an awful presentiment. I took it off to fix a bit of the chain, and couldn't manage it. Then I laid it on that little ledge of your study-table till I could find my book: then he came in, and — yes, I guess he frightened me into forgetting my watch. I haven't thought of it since."

With quaking hearts we went into the study.

The watch was gone! So was my pearl-handled pen-knife, a gold toothpick, a pair of gloves, and a very beautiful gold and enamelled paper-cutter. By this time I was heart-sick.

"He must have taken these things when I was playing — the polished hypocrite!" I said. "If I could get my hands upon him, I'd rope's-end him in spite of my cloth!"

I made a round of visits to my brother clergymen. They had all been victimized. He had played the same *rôle* in each instance, and with such success, that he must have been the richer by a hundred dollars or more.

By setting interested friends to work, I obtained possession of the watch, which had been pawned; but money, or birds, or man, I never saw again.

CHAPTER XIII.

"Some stubborn natures are willing that wrong should be spoken of them rather than make all right, even by a sign."

"I WISH you would call round and see my wife. Tilly has taken a fancy that she is sick."

Tom Tracy said this in his careless fashion, as he stood in the shadow of the chancel one Sunday afternoon.

"Tilly is a little notional now and then," he added, playing with his watch-chain: "women all are, I suppose, particularly when they have no hobbies. I wish my wife would take to district-visiting, or even a Sunday-school class. As it is, she has nothing to do but to keep the house nice, and help my little girl in her sewing. When she goes, I don't know what will become of Tilly."

"Wives are a good deal what we make them," I said. "When the children go, the husbands must redouble their attentions."

I looked at him as he stood there, supremely

handsome, his cold, clear-cut features, over which no ripple of emotion stirred, reminding me of the classic statues of antiquity, and wondered what was passing under that fine, passionless exterior. Surely this man, with not one sensuous feature, could be neither tempter nor tempted in his keen encounter with life, the strange experiences that sometimes surrounded him by reason of his calling.

"Yes: but" — then he placed his lips together, cast a penetrating glance at me — "a man can't be forever at home," he added, evidently changing the sentence which had all but escaped him. "Shall I tell Tilly you will come round?" he queried, his voice grown a little hard, and his eyes a little brighter.

"Tell her she may expect me to-morrow."

I watched him moving down the aisle: his imposing figure, and graceful walk and bearing, would have arrested my attention anywhere; but now all his graces seemed heightened, and his manliness was doubly attractive. I was studying him.

"At all events, the choir were gone," I said to myself: the siren had not enchained him, for that night at least. I should be able to make the promised visit with a lighter heart.

Jenkins had put out the lights, and I went into the study to finish my paper. Presently the door opened, and Dolly peeped in. How happy she looked! Her eyes were laughing with joy and sweetness.

"Come in," I said, "you and Mr. Ravaillac. Of course you are together."

"I am only too happy," said the Frenchman in his precise English, showing himself, and entering.

"Your choir staid late, didn't it?" queried Dolly.

"No: it went early," I said.

"But we just met Mr. Tom Tracy and Mrs. Stanley," said Dolly. "They got into a car as we got out."

"Yes; and I had a linguistic battle," said the Frenchman, with flashing eyes.

"Truly you did," laughed Dolly; "but the car went while you were fighting it. Mr. Tracy will call you out if you are not careful."

"And it is that I will give him what satisfaction he asks."

"We don't fight duels in our country," I said: but my heart felt like lead in my bosom. She — that woman — had been waiting for him during all the time of my conference with him.

I said nothing to Hester about it, but looked forward to my approaching visit with dread.

It was early when I called at the Tracys. The neat maid had just laid the mat on the broad marble step, and she held the door for me to enter.

"How beautiful a home!" I thought, as my feet sank in the rich, thick carpets, and I looked about on the walls, perfect in their wealth of color, in brackets, pictures, vases.

Presently I was ushered up-stairs. Mrs. Tracy's colorless face was the first thing that met my eyes. She was sitting up in a great velvet bed-chair, and there was something like the pallor of death in her countenance. I could not help displaying my astonishment.

"You are very kind," she said, holding out her hand languidly, "very good and kind."

"I did not think, from what Mr. Tracy said, to find you like this," I said unguardedly.

"Tom doesn't know." Her lips quivered through a wavering smile.

"Tom should know!" I said impulsively, and then paused, finding myself on the horns of a dilemma. She had as yet confided nothing to me, though I was her priest, and ready enough to be, in one sense, her confessor. I never could abide confidences, even by the sick-bed; but my calling made it often incumbent upon me to hear the secret burdens of many a bleeding heart.

"O sir!" she said, "I beseech you, help me if you can!"

"What can I do?" I asked softly.

"Save him!"

"You mean your husband?"

"Not so much for my sake as for his. And yet, my heart is breaking. Sometimes I feel the very strings snap."

She gave living action to the speech by a most expressive gesture.

"If I only knew how!" I said helplessly.

"Has he told you nothing?" It would have been affectation to ask her what she meant.

"That is what is killing me. He tells me nothing. He only laughs, or answers with a jest. I implore, I pray, I weep. He laughs. Cruel, cruel!"

"Are you angry with him when you talk?" I asked, hap-hazard.

"Angry! One can't be angry with Tom. Tom is so lovable!"

She looked afar off, as if she saw the lost idol of her youth.

"O sir! I wish I could be angry. And, if I could, he would still smile." Then in a lower voice, and with an expression of agony, —

"It can't be that he *loves* her!"

Then, in still more solemn tones, —

"What have I ever done that he should forget me? Nothing, but worship him. God knows, that, if it is really for his happiness, I wish to die."

"It would not be for his happiness," I said sternly; "but it might be for his punishment."

"No, no! I would have him happy," she exclaimed, bursting into tears. "Let me bear all the sorrow. I wonder, if he laid me in the grave, would the old love come back."

Then, after a long pause, —

"*She* will be the murderer! Oh, she must have used many arts to entrap him! I would have trusted him all my life. He might have left me for years, and I would have trusted him. What do you think is the magic she uses? I don't know but I would even stoop to borrow of her." Then, with a terrible flashing of the eyes, "I do not blame him — I blame her. At *her* door my death will lie!"

"Come, let us reason," I said, for the scene was becoming too painful. "You must not give up: dying would not mend the matter. Can you not think of something — some magic of human love? When he comes home, you say you do not reproach him?"

"Never! I beg, I entreat, I pray: he is always the same. He will tell me nothing, though I should be dying at his feet."

"Perhaps if you pretended not to notice him, went with him to the rehearsals, insisted on your right as a wife to his husbandly attentions" —

She looked at me intently.

"Do you think I am marble?" she said. "Why, the first time I saw that woman look at him with her wicked eyes, I could have strangled her! I saw him once place her shawl on her shoulders — yet I have seen him do that hundreds of times, to the ladies of our household, or acquaintances, or even strangers. What did I care? I loved him better for it; but there came a silent, swift, invisible dagger, that smote me through and through at sight of that simple attention — to *her!* It took the strength out of my heart, and it has never come back. Don't ask me to go near her — to act the spy on him. Trouble would come of it — sore, bitter trouble."

"What, then, do you propose to do?" I asked.

She turned her head wearily away.

"I must die, I suppose," she said, in a pitiful voice; and I could see how her sorrow had sapped the energy of her life, and it might be that death was the only way out.

"It may not be as bad as you imagine," I said.

"I imagine nothing bad — of him! That woman is pitiless: she would rob me of my husband. She holds her finger on my heart, and she knows her power."

"Shall I speak to Mr. Tracy?"

"Oh, if you only would! say something — but oh! say it *so* kindly! His temperament is a strange one. If he would only say, 'Tilly, I don't care for her,' — just those few words, — I'd never think of it again. But he won't. He just laughs, and treats me like a child. I feel myself belittled, undervalued. He believes me silly, notional, jealous. O Heavens! and I am a woman, and his wife! It is very hard!"

"Then, you will leave the matter in my hands?"

She looked up, an imploring expression in her pale, beautiful face.

"You will be gentle with him? You will try to win his confidence? If he says one word to you that will exonerate him — but I know I can trust you. I will leave the matter in your hands."

I left Mrs. Tracy with added respect for herself, and a cold contempt of her husband. Many a new-filled grave have I come from with a lighter heart. In my short course of ministration, I had never seen such agony as this. It depressed me, followed, enveloped me.

Hester rallied me upon my nervousness, and Dolly's beautiful eyes followed me with loving sympathy. If I had told Hester, it would have lessened the burden; but I was unconsciously following Tom Tracy's example. Why should

I trouble her? It was not in her power, I thought, to give me aid in these vexatious matters. But it was. I was simply draining my own strength, and I do not think that even prayer gave me the help her counsel might have done.

The following day Tom Tracy came to my study to consult me about the music for the coming Christmas.

I went over the list he held, revised it, and then with a sinking heart fortified myself as best I could for the coming struggle. There was no need.

The man was polished from his hat to his boot-toes, keen as his own practice, and as slippery as if he had been born a native of the jungles, with fangs and rattles.

"By the way, I called on Mrs. Tracy yesterday, Tom," I said.

"Hm! I thought her looking better when I went home. Thanks!"

"But, Tom — you are not aware, perhaps — I consider her a very sick woman."

"She may be," said Tom; "but the doctor doesn't think so."

"Doctors don't always understand the state of a patient. For instance " —

He looked at me, calm as a statue.

"It is not always the body that is suffering. There are ills beyond that."

"I have heard so," he said simply. "Something that brings on hysterics sometimes."

I clinched my teeth. The fellow either could not or would not understand. What should I say to enlighten him?

"Your wife sent for me, to tell me, as her pastor, a matter that weighs heavily on her mind. Do you happen to know of any trouble that interferes with her happiness?"

"I do not," he replied stolidly.

"You will pardon me if I speak plainly," I said, feeling the gravity of the situation more and more keenly, though his utter indifference goaded me on.

"I should be most happy if you are in my wife's confidence, better acquainted with her trials than I am, to listen to the plainest kind of speech."

His undisguised sarcasm stung me. I lost my temper.

"Your attentions to Mrs. Stanley are very marked," I said, without more circumlocution. "Others have seen it besides myself. Two or three of the vestry have noticed it."

"What do they say?" he asked, after a brief pause, during which his face was as immobile as ever.

"I decline to state, just now," was my answer.

"What do *you* say?" he asked, without the alteration of a feature.

"That I am satisfied you are doing yourself a great wrong."

"What does my wife say?" he then queried, his face flushing slightly.

I thought of all her agony, all her heroism, all her tenderness for him, as she had pleaded with me not to be harsh.

"Your wife says she cannot lose your love and live."

He frowned slightly.

"*What in the world makes women such fools?*" He spoke musingly and slowly, as if to himself. "Tilly knows she irritates me if she doubts me, and yet she will persist in this causeless jealousy."

"Causeless!" I exclaimed.

"Of a man who looks at almost every thing from a judicial stand-point, yes. I know what I am about. Tilly must not meddle with my business, neither, with all due deference to your ministerial duties, must you. If my wife eases her mind by confession, or whatever she may call it, to her pastor, well and good: I don't object. Neither do I choose to give my reasons for every trifling attention I show to another lady. Must I bother her with all my law-cases? I have several lady clients. Tilly must learn to trust me, to be more of a woman, and less an unreasoning child. I don't choose to carry shop home to my wife; and she ought to know it, and thank me for it."

"But why not enlighten her in this particular case if it is *all* business? It would not derogate from your dignity as a man, and would certainly be more to your credit as a husband."

He answered me with a home-thrust. With his fine gray eyes searchingly fixed on mine, he asked, —

"*Do you tell your wife every thing?*"

For an instant I felt weak and helpless. The sword had struck home. Instantly, upon the canvas of my memory, started forth the face of Miriam, reproachful, affectionate, passionate, sad, by turns. There was certainly no distinct parallel between the two cases, yet for a moment I felt the sense of guilt for an offence that was not venial, for I had never wavered in the truest allegiance to Hester; while this man could smile serenely, though he must be conscious that the weal or woe of a human soul hung upon his decision.

But there was the question he had thrust in my face; and it recalled my own arrogant assumptions of manly superiority, my often expressed convictions, that, as head of the wife, the husband has no call to confer in any matter, save what may seem good in his judgment, with his second and often better self.

"Perhaps not as much as I should," was my reply; "but if I saw her health departing, her body losing its vigor, her heart breaking, for lack of the confidence she may feel to be her right, I think I should, even if it amounted to the confession of sin."

"You speak like a parson," he said half angrily. "And you do not know the facts of the case: they are not to be whispered, only into the ears of one's lawyer. Professional men must have secrets, even from their wives: some of these they must carry, even to the grave. It is an unhappy chance, perhaps, that one's clients are beautiful and young, as well as unfortunate. It is also unfortunate that self-constituted spies transmute what they see and hear into their own base metal, and then circulate the coin. I am quite aware that I have been followed. I am also aware that some false friend has written to Tilly, making the case out to suit her own depraved convictions. And if my wife chooses to believe such trash — why, she must e'en do it. I shall not try to enlighten her. I will not stoop so low!"

His lip quivered with suppressed passion, and his brow lowered. For the first time I read in his face the power to do evil and the will to conceal it.

"Then, you will not by a word put an end to your wife's distress, even anguish?"

"I swear I will not," he said, in a tone of suppressed fury: then, evidently feeling that he had gone too far, his face dazzled with a smile that was all sweetness and sunshine.

"I am very impetuous sometimes," he said: "you must pardon me, and excuse my abrupt departure. I have an engagement — *with Mrs. Stanley* — at twelve."

He bowed, turned on his heel, and walked down the aisle towards the door, firing this audacious shot at me as an earnest of his unalterable will.

"Perhaps it is all right," I said to myself. "These conferences behind the choir-curtain are safer than at the office or at her home. She may be applying for a divorce, and have reasons for wishing it to be kept secret. After all, his wife's jealous fears may be without foundation, and his anger may be that of a just man wrongly accused. I wonder what Hester will think of it."

For the first time almost in my life, I felt my helplessness, and longed for my wife's co-operation, — the expression of her judgment, instinct, whatever subtle force it is that makes woman judge and jury in special cases. I had but poor consolation to carry to Tom's wife; and I was half angry that it devolved upon me to see her, and state the success, or non-success rather, of my interview.

When I went into the house, Hester and Dolly were talking something over very softly.

Hester's aunt, Miriam's mother, was dead.

CHAPTER XIV.

"Flowers for the bridal,
Flowers for the dead."

THE news had just come.
Hester was very quiet, but in this case grief was impossible. She had never quite loved her aunt Hope, though very fond of her cousin Miriam.

"We have been wondering what poor Miriam will do," said Hester softly. "And, if I were you, I would go there right away. I am sure *she* would not want any one else but you. Tell her I will come again this evening. I have just been there, and mamma and papa are doing every thing that needs to be done."

"But — will it not be better for me to wait till you go?" I said.

"Why, of course one's clergyman is expected to call immediately in such trouble as this," said Hester, looking up, some surprise in her glance. "I'm afraid aunt Hope was so unfortunate in her temperament, that you visit her sins on poor cousin Miriam, and that she is not a favorite of yours. But she is very different from her mother."

"Perhaps I had better go," I said — "if she will see me."

"I think one always wants to see one's clergyman," said Hester.

I took my hat and cane mechanically, and went forth on this very unpleasant duty. The exercise would do me good, even if Miriam declined to see me. On the road I tried to forget the unpleasant character of my last interview with her, and stopped for the purpose of examining a bit of stone jutting out from the rest. In bending over to see more plainly, my eye followed an object that glittered, half buried in the ground. Another moment, and I held in my hand a valuable solitaire diamond earring of antique shape and pattern. The gold was dim and stained, but the stone was remarkably clear and brilliant. Wondering much at this strange incident, I placed the ornament in my pocket, and proceeded on to the cottage of the Hopes.

Alas! the shroud seems to envelop all material things when death comes into any household. The quietude, the crape on the door, the closed blinds, the general mournful aspect of the surroundings, extending even to the trees and the flowers in the garden, seem a commentary on the fleeting value of all that lives. I rang the bell. A colored servant came to the door, and ushered me into the parlor. Flowers in baskets and on stands saluted my senses. Will it be believed? I had already become indifferent to the delicious fragrance of every flower that breathes the air of the charnel-house. Seeing them heaped up on coffins, placed in the hands of the dead, wreathed about their cold faces, lying on their pulseless breasts, flung into their gloomy graves, clustered over the green-sward, has sickened me. Thus, when I enter the bright homes of my parishioners, the perfume of the heavily scented roses, so grateful to the senses of most people, is a disturbing element to me; and the last funeral rises up to haunt me with all its dread, disturbing recollections.

My mother-in-law sat there, sorting the flowers. She looked rather cheerful, though at sight of me she drew down the corners of her mouth.

"I was thinking of you," she said, "and wondering why you didn't come. Poor sister Lydia held out a long time: she had a terrible will. And I'm glad the flowers came in, she was so fond of flowers! Pity you couldn't have been with her at the last, but she was called in the night. It seemed sudden, too; and we none of us know," etc. I spare the reader all the moralizing I can. I hate it myself.

"How does Miriam bear it?" was my first question.

"Very bravely. There is a good deal of strength in Miriam's character. She resisted as long as she could keep the enemy at bay. When all was over; she was very calm. Miriam has always seemed to me like a daughter: indeed, she is more like me than Hester ever was."

This was a gratifying piece of intelligence. I had been slowly hardening my heart against Miriam, partly perhaps because I had unwittingly done her a wrong, partly because of some glimpses I had caught of her character. More in love than ever with my Hester, I was glad Miriam did not resemble her.

Presently a slow step sounded: the door opened, and there stood Miriam. Evidently the maid had not told her of my coming; for she started and drew back as she saw me, and the color rolled in a wave all over her face. Otherwise she was unchanged. A curious expression, like an electric flash, suffused her countenance as she drew herself up, and came quietly forward.

"So your mother has left us," I said.

"Yes:" the tears welled up to her eyes;

"but I ought not to mourn, she was such a sufferer."

"And while I admire her resignation," said my mother-in-law, "I cannot agree with Miriam in her decision against full mourning."

"I am but following out mamma's own suggestion," said Miriam, her beautiful dark eyes still suffused. "I always dress in black; but crape"—she shuddered. "I should die muffled up in crape."

"Your decision does your judgment credit," I said. "I condemn crape. Let our mourning be of the heart, not of the garments."

"Fudge!" ejaculated Hester's mother contemptuously. "There is nothing more becoming or fashionable. I'd swathe her in it if I had my way, particularly with her style of beauty. And it looks so *proper* at a church funeral."

"Mamma will be buried from the house," said Miriam softly.

"Now, Miriam, you do provoke me. If I had thought my sister was to have a commonplace funeral, like any poor parishioner, I declare I wouldn't have stirred out of the house."

"But I must follow out mamma's last wishes," said Miriam imploringly; "and that was one of them."

"Well, I am very sorry;" and she grouped the

flowers with nervous energy. "Lydia always was full of whims, even at her best. Why, this room won't hold fifty people; and *our* friends are legion. If it had been a large, stylish house, now, the effect would have been different. She must have known she was going against my wishes. Besides, it looks as if she held a grudge against the rector."

Miriam turned deadly pale. I feared she was going to faint. But she conquered the weakness, and her color came back.

"Mamma's ideas of things changed very much during her sickness," she said quietly.

"I hope she didn't say how she wanted to be laid out," muttered my mother-in-law.

"Yes, she did; and I have given instructions — in white," said Miriam.

The woman let fall her flowers.

"If she had had a grudge against *me*," she said angrily, "she couldn't have more crossed my wishes; and she with a full suit of black satin! I declare I sha'n't be able to look folks in the face. One would think we had been reared in the dark ages. Everybody who is buried *decently* is buried in good clothes." Saying this, she left the room.

Miriam smiled faintly.

"My aunt is a great stickler for fashion, even with the dead," she said sadly.

I attempted a few words of consolation, but they seemed to fall flat. Miriam was silent. One thought was dominant in my mind. Her mother had disliked and defied me, and my presence was distasteful to her. She only listened on sufferance. I rose to depart, and held out my hand. She gave me hers, but only for a touch, drawing it away as if it stung her.

"Cousin Miriam," I said, "are we not friends?"

Turning partly away, she whispered something that was inaudible to me; turned again, cast upon me a look that I should have resented had she given me time, and hurried from the room, apparently convulsed with grief.

This was pleasant, and I heartily wished Hester's cousin at the antipodes. So poor and weak a creature was not exactly formidable as an enemy, but even weakness has its weapons when guided by impulse or passion.

Hester was an eager questioner when I returned home. How did Miriam meet me? what was her mother doing? To stay the tide of her unreasoning yet natural curiosity, I brought forth the earring I had found.

Hester seized it with a little cry.

"Where did you find it? I have its counterpart up-stairs in my jewel-box. The rings belonged to my mother's great-grandmother! O

Hal, what a lucky fellow you are! I have so many times wished for this, so valuable as an heirloom, you know; and now I can wear them both. Mother will be so delighted. How did it come in your possession?"

I explained.

"I'm so glad! We always thought poor Prinny stole it. Prinny was a half-witted girl, who used to come with her mother to do the scrubbing when I was a child. I remember there was a terrible time, and how meek the poor woman was under it all. I remember also hearing afterwards that people thought mother was very hard towards her, and also that when the girl died, a few years ago, she declared that God would show those rich, purse-proud people that she was innocent. Now, you know, this proves it; and we must go at once to Susan Coles, and tell her about it."

To Susan Coles I gladly accompanied my wife that very night. The old woman lived in a little tumble-down cabin on the edge of the county road. I shall never forget her look when Hester told the story of finding the earring.

"My poor Prinny! do you hear? do you see?" she said, in accents of almost holy joy. Then, turning to us with dignity, "I knew my child wasn't a thief. And I don't believe you ever thought it, Miss Hester," she added.

"No, Susan: I always pitied you," said Hester, "and kept a lookout for you."

"That you have, Miss Hester: the Lord bless you for it!" said the old woman.

From there to the professor's house. Hester's mother heard the story through, and looked at the ring.

"I'm not so sure Prinny didn't take it, now," she said serenely. "I should like to know how you can prove that she didn't throw it where you found it."

"That's mother!" said Hester to me afterwards: "once she makes up her mind, no earthly power can change it. I have noticed that trait in our Frenchman;—and, by the way, don't you see how much he likes Dolly? I'm quite sure he will marry her, and take her to Paris on their bridal tour. And his sister is coming over to America,—the sister he loves so dearly. It does me good to hear him talk about her. By the way, I don't think you have seen her picture."

She went to a little cabinet, and brought me a picture of a beautiful woman, dressed in black, with soft laces at wrists and throat.

"That is the French colonel's wife: and they have a little son, a darling little boy; she is going to bring him with her. It seems as if he would go wild with happiness when he talks about them. 'Only three weeks,' he says, over and over, 'and I shall see *mon ange* Elise!' I have become so much interested in her, myself, that I know I shall like her as a friend. And she can talk English too. He showed me a letter very fairly written, indeed, for a French woman who has never left France. There was an allusion to Madame the Comtesse de Berri; which shows, you know, that they have good society."

I was very glad for little Dolly, the more so as my wife seemed to vouch for the respectability of Ravaillac. But I had made up my mind that I should ask for something more than his word for it.

CHAPTER XV.

"To make pretence, look large, and cry up my ancestors, sirs!"

MRS. HOPE was buried, the cottage let to a widow who taught school, and Miriam became an inmate of the professor's home. Marguerite was well pleased with the arrangement, as she had never liked her school; and Miriam was quite competent to instruct the child in all the common branches.

I seldom saw Miriam, except when she came to church; and then the professor's pew was nearer the choir than the chancel: and she never remained after services, even to speak to Hester, who declared, that, of late, Miriam was an enigma.

One day Jenkins brought an ordinary paper tablet, which he said he had found one Sunday, a little way from the rector's pew. At first I placed it on my desk, for I was busy. A fresh instalment of the Tracy-Stanley scandal had just been brought to my hearing, and it pained me deeply. Mrs. Tracy never came to church now, and her daughter but seldom. That very day Hester had fixed upon for a visit to Mrs. Tracy.

I had not yet learned the art of resting, but took plunges from one sort of work into another, till both brain and heart were wearied with continuous labor. Added to this, the wear and tear of sympathy with some extraordinary phases of mental suffering among the members of my congregation made even my sleep uncertain. Mrs. Dickory was another worry incidental to my discomfort. She would persist in bringing her three restless, nervous children to church, dressed in the most *outre*, outlandish manner, and parading them on the front seat just opposite the lectern. There she busied herself during the whole service, inspecting their nails and noses, brushing their hair, picking sundry obstructions out of their ears and her own, making eyes at me, and posing in what she thought an attitude of perfect grace, but which was so ridiculous that I sometimes thought I must leave the sacred desk, and turn her and all the young Dickories out of the house. Mr. Dickory never came: they said he did his best work on Sunday. But Mrs. Dickory more than made up for his absence. She was always the last person to leave the church: and she talked incessantly, whoever else claimed my attention;

while I had not even the poor privilege of bidding her hold her tongue, but must listen with one ear on her side, and one on the other, where perchance some one else talked and talked.

Of all men, the minister is the most accessible to bores. They come morning, noon, and night, invade his sanctum, smoke his cigars if he uses them, appropriate his time. Under cover of all kinds of charitable plans, religious doubts or enthusiasms, missionary zeal, domestic difficulties, they steal not only his purse, for it often virtually amounts to that, — but his peace of mind, and his well-earned rest. The greater his need of privacy at certain times, the more frequent the interruption, until he cries with St. Paul, "Wretched man that I am, who shall deliver me?" It takes a man of peculiar resources to rid himself of such pests without injury to his reputation as a Christian, or his self-respect as a man.

I had prepared the paper for my sermon after Jenkins had taken his long ears out of my study, when suddenly my eye fell on the tablets. Something in the fine, formal handwriting attracted my attention; and I lifted it, bringing it nearer to me. I looked it over for some indication of the *personnel* of the writer; but there was no name, not even a *nom du plume*. Had I among my congregation an incipient novelist?

Almost before I knew it, my glance ran over the items.

"*Mem.* — The name shall be —   I will find a name later on.

"To be consistent, I must fit in and perfectly dovetail every fact, and make my memory to be unassailable. For this purpose, these facts must be of the utmost completeness.

"There shall be an old family, and it must be that the ancestry shall be studied and traced so carefully that no mistakes can be possible.

"First, then, there is the *grand-mère*, born of noble parents, living at ——, where she was born, as was also my mother. Her home shall be studied, from the tiling on the floors, to the initials on the gable of the house. I shall know even just where the cat sits. I shall answer for the birds and the flowers, their color and their perfume. The chair near the hearth is tapestried: the table is of red satin-wood; and always there is a basket there, filled with colored cottons and wools.

"With that house are connected several stories. Great generals have made it their resort. During the war, it must have been respected and guarded. The grandmother must be small, quick in all her movements, with a very beautiful smile. She must have received her grandchild, when the mother died, as a gift from *le bon Dieu*, and trained him very carefully. Her hair must be snow-white, and her eyes large and dark.

"Then, there must be a sister married from the same house, — and, of course, much older than I am, — to one of the great colonels. She moves to another home, really a palace on some fine boulevard, and is very intimate with the nobility. Her name will be — I will think of her name presently. She is married five years. Her beautiful little child is three years old. Ah! the treasure! the *petit neveu!* One's heart leaps out to him so, the sweet little angel with eyes that win one's love! Yes, that is well conceived, — the sister, the grand colonel, the little nephew. It then remains that I can do what I please with the *dramatis personæ*. I make them, and like puppets I move them. They live, they die, at my command. They have wealth, horses, carriages, servants, as I multiply or lessen them. What a privilege!

"Now for myself!

"If pressed to say why I leave Paris, I have ready a story at my tongue's end.

"I am educated a soldier. I am the son of a French officer, a martinet as well as a military man. Of imposing presence, tall, muscular, of broad shoulders, one of the handsomest of handsome men, very much in love with my mother, very strict and severe with the son, such is my father. I admire, I fear him, but I love him not. He uses to me the strictest discipline. I am punished for the most trifling things. I escape from school to go fishing one day. I am put in solitary confinement one week. I refuse to touch my hat to an old soldier. I am put in irons for one day. These things to invent is easy. I will stock my mind with them, and so set down all I would say, and fortify my memory so as that I never forget.

"Then, as I grow up, I receive a military education. I am put in a French battalion, and I dislike to be deprived of my liberty. At last I have a quarrel. I, second lieutenant, strike my superior, first lieutenant, with my sword. For that I am court-martialed; but, after sentence is passed, I free myself, and immediately fly my country. Ah! beloved France! '*France, I adore thee!*' I cannot see thee for three years! My little grandmother idolizes the only son of her only daughter. Every month I receive presents and letters. On my birthday Elise — yes, I will call her Elise — cables me a message, not forgetting my dear love, whom I idolize, *mon ange*, the beautiful little one above all others of her sex, and whom I would die for. My sister will write me that she longs to embrace me; that she will come to America. I engage for her a room: I look for her coming with ecstasy. Alas! she is ill! She has fallen from her horse: she is very ill — like to die! Thus her visit is put off till later. But she will come — do not her letters tell me so? — *if she lives!* Again she is coming — again she is detained — it may be necessary for her to die. Of that I will decide myself in time. She sends gifts to *mon ange*, gifts of the very finest Paris quality — that can easily be done. She, with my grandmother, will send me money each month. Then, when all is safe — Ah! *when all is safe!* Will that time come? I am required to produce such evidence" —

Here the manuscript ended, and I sat looking at it stupidly. That neat, methodical hand, more like print than pen — I had seen it before, on the notes sent to the house, to little Dolly. What was I to think? Ravaillac must have been the writer; but what motive could underlie the curious invention, if invention it was? Perhaps, after all, it was a mere literary *résumé;* monsieur might be an author; or he might be giving points to Dolly, knowing her to be a writer of fiction. But then, why did this written record correspond so exactly with his present plan of action? Hester had spoken of his sister, showed me her picture; she was the wife of a military man; his description of his grandmother corresponded to the sketch before me; his sister was expected in America; he had engaged rooms for her. I remembered now, Dolly's exhibiting some very beautiful fragments of silk and satin, pieces of dresses in preparation of making for the tour to America. Quite proper that a sister interested in the only brother she had in the world, should be thus intimate in her correspondence. Hester had liked it, and praised her for it. Was my wife's usual acute sense of right and wrong at fault? I had surprised her two or three times studying the Frenchman's face, and once or twice she had gone off into a reverie while talking of him. Did she have forebodings, and yet decline to speak of them, seeing Dolly so very, very happy, so thoroughly in love with her hero?

"It is like the atmosphere of fairy-land," she said to me on one occasion, "to sit where they two are, and look on now and then — sometimes to catch some beautiful ray of love-light. It is idyllic. Who could predict any thing but happiness?"

Meantime my sisters had each had their say. To one and all, the Frenchman was distasteful: they didn't like foreigners; they didn't want Dolly carried off from the home of her kindred, and treated nobody knew how. They usually made prim little calls on us when they came to the city, very seldom remaining over a day. But they came often, as they were getting ready for my sister Belle's marriage; and they were all loud in their praises of Hester's house-keeping. It hurt Dolly that her sisters seemed to have taken so decided a dislike to her lover, but only made her cling to him the closer.

Should I at once confide in Hester? My good genius said "Yes;" but my natural tendency to defer all matters that were not pleasant to some other day, triumphed this time. I placed the tablet in my pocket, fully intending to speak to Hester soon.

CHAPTER XVI.

*"A happy thought, a sweet surprise,
Glad words, and gladder kisses."*

TO find Hester in a storm of angry tears, almost in hysterics, in fact, was an episode in my married life for which I was not prepared.

"Go down to tea without me: I am too thoroughly vexed to eat or drink for a week to come," she said, rising as she spoke, and dabbing her eyes with an expensive bit of flabby muslin.

"Why, Hester, what have I done?" I asked in mild consternation.

"Nothing — only committed the unpardonable offence of being a man!" was her rather irascible and unreasonable answer. "I have been over to Mrs. Tracy's, that's all. It's just abominable, the way that poor woman is being killed by inches! I really think her husband ought to be arrested for murder."

"My dear! are you not rash in your assertion?" I asked.

"No! to marry a woman, and then torture

her, is a crime against God and man. If you had seen that poor heart-broken creature! And yet she could smile. 'It is all over now,' she said, 'and I am glad.' Do you believe she will die?"

"Is she in bed?"

"No; moving about the house, her cheeks like roses; but yet in her eyes there is a look of death. I wish she was more assertive. I'd like to see the man *I* would die for!" with a vindictive little glare and another dab. "It seems she found something — a letter, I think — from that — woman — that creature! the vile thing! she ought to be torn in pieces."

"But what can I do?"

"Don't let *him* sing those holy words Sunday after Sunday. It is blasphemy in the sight of Heaven.

"Yes," I said, "it is blasphemy; but what shall we do about the service?"

"Let the service go. Get the Sunday-school children in the choir, and send that woman off. I'll play the organ till you can get somebody else."

"Is not that going to extremes?"

"No: it is simple justice. Mercy under such circumstances is criminal: forbearance is no longer a virtue. I cannot hear that man sing again."

"I will see about it to-night," I said. "Bathe your eyes, and come down to tea: don't visit your wrath upon my poor unprotected head."

"No, indeed! Thank God that he has given me a true heart that has no vile secrets to hide!" And she shed the last tears on my bosom, held close to my heart. Then we went down-stairs together, she little thinking that I had withheld a secret from her.

Mr. Ravaillac was there. Perhaps my greeting was constrained. He looked at me keenly, then silently backed to a seat near Dolly, who was knitting. We were all rather moody at the tea-table. I had a miserable task before me: Ravaillac was quieter than his wont, Dolly abstracted.

As usual on that evening, the choir practised; and, as usual, the tenor and the organist were the last to leave. I heard them talking together in low tones, but yet could not bring myself to determine in what manner to broach the subject. Still, what my wife had said rung in my ears, — "Don't let him sing those holy words Sunday after Sunday," — and I could not longer brook the seeming inconsistency. I had become almost morbidly nervous by reason of the constant allusions of my friends to this matter. What train of circumstances my plain talk might disclose, I could not conjecture; but I was powerless to prevent it, for my own conscience seconded the decision that Hester wished me to make.

Presently I heard steps coming towards the study.

Another moment, and tall, handsome Tom Tracy stood before me, a paper in his hand.

"I just wanted you to run your eye over this," he said quietly, as he placed the paper before me. It was a list of the anthems, hymns, and *Te Deum* to be sung at Christmas.

"I shall take it to 'The Daily News' on my way to the office to-morrow," he said, as I refolded and handed it to him. "It will probably be out in Saturday-night's paper. That will be time enough, as Christmas comes this year on Sunday."

"You will sing the new *Te Deum*, I suppose," I said, with a view to detaining him; "that is, *if* you sing."

"If I sing! why, of course I shall sing!" he said.

"I don't know, after what I have to say to you," was my reply.

"I hope it is nothing very serious," he remarked, with his soft, sweet smile; but it seemed to me that a harder look came into his face.

"Simply this, Mr. Tracy,—that this flirtation

with Mrs. Stanley has gone too far, if indeed it is nothing more than what that mild word signifies. Several of the wardens have spoken to me; your wife herself is in a most pitiable condition; and, seriously, I must request that in some effectual way the thing be disposed of before you both lose your good name with the public. Believe me, I speak as a friend. I do not want you to become my enemy."

"Then, why do you try to make me your enemy?" Tom Tracy asked, lifting his square shoulders haughtily, and looking me defiantly in the face, while an angry red glowed on each cheek. "There was a time when people said the young minister was flirting with the cousin of his destined wife. I myself knew of your going there six evenings out of the seven. Those who live in glass houses had better not throw stones. I fancy you did not tell your wife of that brief infatuation. Oh! I know all about it, reverend sir — more, perhaps, than you think."

I rose from my seat, angry and white; for I felt the blood rush back upon my heart.

"My wife left her cousin in my care," I said; "but I shall not notice your contemptible speech. You are a married man: Mrs. Stanley is a married woman. You say her husband is cruel to her: have you no pity for your wife, whose heart you are slowly breaking?"

"Tilly must have confidence in me: she knows better," he said sullenly. "If she has a mind to distrust me, and allows her absurd jealousy to master her, she must. I swear I won't humble myself!"

"Is Mrs. Stanley waiting for you?" I asked.

"Mrs. Stanley is probably waiting for me," he said, after a slight pause.

"Let her wait in vain," I said, touching his sleeve with my finger. "Let me plead with you, as a minister of God, to go home to your wife, and let *her* go home to her husband alone. She is not one of the timid sort, believe me; she is not afraid; it is customary with women who support themselves. Think how much happiness you will give your wife! It would hurt you to look into a new-made grave."

That he was touched, I knew by a certain movement of the lip, a contraction of the brow. I followed up my advantage till I thought he would listen to me.

"Perhaps," he said in a low voice, "I may excuse myself;" and with that I had to be content. I could not play the spy, but Jenkins did. He had not, it seems, been far away during the whole interview, and so came to me ten minutes after Tom had gone, and in a stage-whisper, putting his gaunt face and long ears in at the door, said, —

"Muster Tracy seen her home! — got into the car himself, and went past Tolman Square."

Tolman Square was where Tom Tracy lived, where his wife was slowly dying; and I had doubtless made him my pitiless enemy.

Christmas Day came. Never had the church looked more beautiful: never had the sunshine seemed more glorious as it sifted through the stained windows, and painted the walls and the ceilings with the master hand of an artist who never makes mistakes in outline or coloring.

The bell rang, tolled: no sound from the silent organ, no face above the choir-curtains!

Christmas Day, and no service of song! My hand trembled as I turned the pages of the hymnal, and my heart sank within me. My cowardly tenor had deserted me without a word of warning; though doubtless many had been drawn by the advertisement in the evening paper, to hear the new and celebrated *Te Deum*. Never had the old church been so filled: everywhere the faces of my people, everywhere the faces of strangers, mixed and mingled. There was a surfeit of color; every countenance shone in the reflected light; even Mrs. Dickory and her three ill-favored children contrived to look a little like saints on that glorious day: — but what should I do without the Christmas service of song?

Suddenly I heard a subdued murmuring, and then a rustle as of angel's wings. Presently a low, sweet solo stole from the organ through the quiet, and then some pure harmonies, that fell on the hush, and on my perturbed spirit, like voices from the celestial land.

A paper was sent up to me, which I read under cover of my book.

"Go on just the same: we will chant the *Te Deum*. Dolly will sing 'Angels ever bright' at the offertory. We have it all arranged." HESTER."

My trembling soul took courage. I felt like a bird just escaped from the snare of the fowler, and stood erect once more, freed from the burden that had well-nigh conquered me. Then sounded the clear, well-trained voices of the children, thirty of them; and a look of surprise, blended with pleasure, passed from face to face. All the chants, the *Gloria*, the *Te Deum*, passed off in succession with perfect toning and exceptional harmony. Then at the close came Dolly's beautiful soprano voice, faultless and unfaltering, in "Angels ever bright and fair." The service of song was a triumph. One after another of my parishioners came forward at the close. "What a surprise you have given us! what a charming service! Whose was that birdlike voice in the solo? How can we thank you enough?"

Hester was radiant.

"Well!" she exclaimed breathlessly, as I met her in the parlor. For answer I caught her to my heart.

"Dolly and I talked it over," said Hester, after she had blushingly disentangled her curls from one of my coat-buttons. "I was afraid Tracy would play you that trick. As the Quakers say, it was borne in upon me; so, fearful that you might be left in the lurch, Dolly and I called upon some of our best singers in the Sunday school, and we have been practising ever since, at the house of Mayor Proctor."

"But you might have told me," I said.

"If we had been sure — but of course we had no hint of how matters stood. It was simply my prescience, or whatever you might call it. We all met together in the parsonage after the ringing of the bell, and Jenkins came in from time to time to report progress. Then, as the bell tolled, and still they came not, we forthwith proceeded to action. How did you like my voluntary?"

"Coming, as it did, on that terrible blank of expectation, it was simply delicious," I said, "I grew to the stature of a man at once. Before that, I was not conscious of any thing but a stinging defeat, and a curious sense of having brought it upon myself. And then the sweet voices of the children! Truly it was a fitting service of song for the beautiful Christmas."

"I have another surprise," said Hester; and, throwing open the folding-doors, there were my sisters, her parents, Miriam, and the children who had so lightened the labors of the holy day.

Dinner was a feast of good things, and a happier company never gathered together under the roof of the rectory. Still, if I must confess it, my pleasure was strangely marred by the proximity of Miriam, who was seated at my left hand. Why should she be a disturbing presence? but it was always so.

"Did you notice the tenor?" asked Hester, when we talked it over.

"I heard one of the sweetest of tenor voices, but cannot imagine whose it was," I said.

"Mr. Ravaillac helped us," was Hester's rejoinder. "Indeed, we have been greatly indebted to him all the way through."

"Why is he not here?" I asked. "I should like to thank him."

"He had a cablegram from his sister: it was brought into church just after service," said Hester. "He would not tell us what it was, but looked very much agitated, and said he must go to his boarding-house at once. I hope nothing has happened."

"Oh!"

I was mentally reading a line from the little block Jenkins had found.

"*I make them, and like puppets I move them. They live and die at my command.*"

"But he might have helped us eat our Christmas dinner!"

"Lucky for you, my dear, that I could spare my cook. You never would have hired a woman that could brown a turkey like that, could she, professor?"

"It was a perfect success," said the professor, folding his napkin.

CHAPTER XVII.

*"Of all sad bridals, that was saddest:
Of all sad brides, the saddest she."*

TOM TRACY was lost to us. In less than a month he was the leader of another choir where Mrs. Stanley played the organ. People cried "Shame!" and then perhaps forgot it, but we were denied that consolation. His wife was a member of my church, as was also her daughter.

One day, a week after Christmas, I was called for, to go to Mrs. Tracy The messenger was her own servant, whose eyes were red with weeping.

"Is your mistress worse?" I asked.

"I don't know, sir; but it's a wedding ceremony they want, I believe. Miss Tracy is going to be married."

"Certainly she is going to be married," said Hester; "but I have heard them say repeatedly, that the ceremony was to be in the church. You know she has a splendid outfit, and her wedding-dress is a miracle of lace and embroidery. Mrs. Tracy showed it to me the last time I was there. They have been taking great pains with the invitations. It must be a mistake of the maid."

"You will go with me," I said; and Hester, laughing at my anxious face, ran to get her wraps.

"Oh, I am chilly!" said Hester, shuddering, as we neared the door. "Look for me: is the handle craped?"

I assured her there was nothing on the door.

"I seemed to see it," she said, drawing a long breath, then grasped my arm more tightly. The door was opened by a strange woman.

"You will go up-stairs," she said solemnly. The atmosphere was stifling. I felt myself beginning to tremble with some vague fear. The door to the right was open: it led into Mrs. Tracy's room. We heard hasty footsteps, and saw the flitting of a white-draped figure: we heard heavy sobs.

There was but a moment between that and the sight of Mrs. Tracy breathing heavily on her great white bed. Tom stood at the head, and she had grasped and now held his hand convulsively. Sometimes she held it up to her pillow, and pressed her cheek against it.

"Don't worry, dear: I am very glad," she said, looking up into his cold, handsome face, with a glance that could not be described, yearning, pitiful, wistful, as if to call his very soul to account, hear his confession, and forgive.

Presently the women at the door-way made a movement, and in their midst stood Marie in her bridal robes; Charley Orowin, her betrothed, also in his bridal suit, closely following.

The girl was now composed, but her face was all stained with her sorrow. Tom never lifted his eyes. They were fastened to the face of the wife he had wronged.

"I swear I will not humble myself," seemed written on every line of his countenance.

"Come, Marie, darling," said the dying woman; "and, O Charley! before I give her to you, promise me — I won't ask you to swear it — that you will be true to her as long as she lives."

"I do solemnly promise," he said in a low voice, broken by emotion.

"Every thing is ready," said the dying woman, turning her eyes upon me; and, at a gesture, I read the marriage service.

The scene was a picture too painful for portrayal. When all was over, there was utter silence; but on the face of the mother came a smile that seemed to transfigure the whole countenance. I never saw any thing so beautiful, in all my experiences of death-beds.

"Dear, dear Tom! it's all right now. Don't mind what I said last night: I didn't want to go then. I shall never forget what you have been to me since you took me out of school, a simple child of fifteen. You were father, brother, every thing; and I thank you, I bless you!"

He threw himself on his knees, his head buried in the pillow, within reach of her hand; and she let her fingers stray through the shining locks, gazing on them with a dying pride.

Was the man not yet willing to humble himself, when it was brought home to him at last that he had broken her heart?

She turned to me with a smile, then looked at him, then at me. It was a mute question, and I understood it; but he had put himself beyond my help. Standing there, I loathed the sight of him as a Christian man should not.

After I had ministered according to the rules of the Church, and spoken a few words of comfort, I left the room. Passing the parlor, downstairs, I caught sight of a long, shining train, and then of the new bride weeping on the breast of the new husband.

Sad beginning of bridal happiness!

We were going by, when the groom called my wife.

"Can you think of any thing to comfort her?" he asked, as Marie lifted her face from his shoulder.

"No, Charley; nobody can comfort me; don't ask her: she knows — the — cause of it all;" and again she fell, almost fainting, into her husband's arms. It was a terrible lesson to him, needed or not.

Presently she lifted her white face.

"I wouldn't believe it," she said; "but the doctor says she has been dying for days — think of it! for days! — and knowing it all the time."

"She will be happier, dear," said Hester.

"I don't know," she retorted, almost fiercely: "perhaps the torture will follow her. It was more idolatry than love. Father has been her God — and mine too," she added bitterly, "till now. Now" — and she clinched her hands — "I hate him!"

"Hush, dear," said her husband gently.

She turned upon him such a look, as she said, —

"He has murdered my mother!"

We took our leave, for the scene was too painful.

"Did you see that picture was gone from the bracket?" Hester asked.

"What picture?"

"Of *that* Mrs. Stanley! I can imagine poor

little Marie snatching it from its place, and grinding it to pieces under her feet. I would!"

"My dear Hester! it seems to me that the presence of death ought to dispel all these baleful human passions," I said.

She looked up at me.

"Do you feel so very much like an angel?" she asked.

"Not exactly," I was forced to reply, with a laugh; for her inimitable expression provoked it.

"If you did, I should consider you a sort of monster," Hester went on. "Here is that woman dying,—and she may be only one of many,—when one word from her husband, spoken in time, would have saved a beautiful human soul, and a home such as few men have. *And he knows it!* I don't wonder his child hates him. O Hal! you poor boy! I never realized before, how many miserable things you are called to see. I mean to be such a good, helpful wife to you!"

"You are all I could ask." She hugged my arm, and I thought I heard a sob.

Early in the morning Mrs. Tracy's girl came round. We all knew what that meant.

"She died so sweetly, though she wandered, miss, toward the last." We heard of that afterwards.

"Tom, dear, don't put her shawl on! don't look at her so! If you knew the pain that comes at my heart — just like a dagger thrust in and in!"

"And so until the very last," a neighbor said.

Thus endeth this short, sad record. How many husbands whose eyes chance to read these pages would dare invoke such dying pangs?

Did he change? I met him a few weeks after. He was as cold, as handsome, as graceful as ever. He did not have the audacity to bow to me.

They say he talks of "Tilly" sometimes, sometimes says he misses her.

That is all. Mrs. Stanley has procured her divorce.

What next?

CHAPTER XVIII.

*"So skilfully her woes proclaimed,
You could not see her tears, and keep your purse."*

"THE natural limit of mankind lies between a cradle and a grave."

"Please don't sermonize," said Hester, looking up from her sewing.

"I only want to convince your father, my dear," was my reply.

"But his hair is gray; and, after all, what does it signify what men believe, if they live right?"

"There!" said the old professor triumphantly: "my girl hasn't forgotten her old training, if she did marry a minister!"

"But I contend that it *does* signify," I retorted.

"Rousseau, about the middle of the last century (1764), ushered in what is known as the Sentimental Philosophy; i.e., that human nature is perfectly good from the start. Bad systems of education, alone, were answerable for bad government and bad communities.

"One of Rousseau's books elaborates this idea, as you know, on the plan of perfect seclusion from outside influence, either of established customs, forms of conduct, current opinions, or recognized creeds of religion. Sweep these all aside, and let pure nature assert itself amid merely pleasant and agreeable surroundings, and this would bring a millennium of natural goodness that would captivate the world."

"Yes: I like the old fellow," said the professor, stroking his white beard. "Think he was right, too, in a degree."

"But, my dear father, this was the prolific philosophy of France amid the horrors of the French Revolution, — a philosophy that nursed the idea of evil as a necessary outgrowth of prevalent opinions and institutions, — a philosophy that lauded the high character of human nature for itself alone, that made its own religion, in which mankind was the chief deity to be worshipped, in which all divisions of race, class-interest, language, climate, association, disappeared, and one scheme of universal love embraced all mankind, as one people under one law. Such a philosophy was capable of instituting a reign of terror by exciting the worst elements of society into war against the invaders of their common rights, who guided the nation, and fostered those symptoms of religion and education which moulded and influenced the rising generation of the land.

"Such a philosophy," I continued, not allowing the professor to interrupt, while Hester held up both hands in mock supplication, "has been the prolific mother of the dreaded Commune, and the more stubborn children of Nihilism. It is the patron of the dynamite fiend. Take away from life its safeguard of discipline and order, its sufferings and its sorrows, its struggles and its labors, and nature would sink into ruin and devastation. Somebody says, 'That which keeps men patient under the evil of this present state of things, is the idea of their necessity, the notion, indistinct, but still real in their minds, that injustice and disorder are fundamental in this visible system of our life. We must be made perfect through suffering."

"Please keep your exhortations for the chancel," said Hester, laughing and frowning. "You can't make me believe that poor Mrs. Tracy was destined to suffer in the way she did, from all eternity."

"That involves another view of the case," said I, as the door opened.

"O Mr. Ravaillac!" cried Hester, "I'm so thankful you have come! You have saved us from a twenty-minutes' sermon."

The professor arose, made a formal bow, protested he had finished his pipe, and left the house. He had just come over to ask Hester to call at her old home that evening, as her mother was not feeling well; and he did not like monsieur.

Ravaillac always seemed to bring with him a wave from some superior region, where people never did ordinary work, or thought ordinary thoughts. Trim, elegant, modest, he was the picture of a modern Apollo, faultlessly dressed. His ardent, sanguine temperament always gave one the impression that he was at peace with himself and all the world.

For some reason, — no doubt, the little tablet that I had locked in my study sufficiently explained it, — I had felt towards him, since reading them, an instinctive antagonism; and he knew it. I could see, by the rapid side-glances he cast towards me now and then, that he was aware of the change in my feelings; but there he stood, handsome, and smiling around at us all.

Presently the door opened; and Dolly's radiant face, framed in some creamy lace-work, — or it might be wool, — broke in upon the silence. How transcendently beautiful she looked, in her pretty opera-wraps! I could not fail to perceive that the glance with which he turned to her was genuine worship. Was I allowing this thing to go too far? I watched him dexterously unfolding her fleecy shawl, so that its texture might catch the warmth of the fire before he placed it over her shoulders. And her face! was it not an index of a rare, true love?

"Very strange," I said, when they had gone, and Hester and I had the cosey room all to ourselves, "that fellow does not get his references from Paris. It is now three months, and he has done nothing but promise."

"That fellow!" exclaimed Hester with emphasis, looking her surprise.

"Well, candidly, I do not like his dilly-dallying with serious matters. He tells a tolerably straight story, but how are we to know? It would be foolish indeed to rely upon his mere say-so."

"Perhaps," said Hester thoughtfully; "and yet there is such an air of sincerity in all he does and says, that I can't for the life of me persist in doubting him."

"Persist!"

"Well, I have had my doubts," Hester went on, smiling to herself; "but it seems to me Nature has set her sign-manual on him as a prince. He certainly has a splendid position. Mr. Whitby trusts him with the most intricate matters of business, and is really going to send him to Paris on his wedding-trip."

"His wedding-trip! Good Heavens! what is Dolly thinking of? Is the time set?"

"Why, not that I know of," said Hester. "I mean, whenever it is to be, of course. I think they are not yet engaged. Dolly has told him that he must come to you."

"I am glad Dolly is so sensible," I said, drawing a long breath. "Yes, yes — that will be time enough."

"What do you mean?" Hester asked.

"I mean, to speak plainly about his references, and his means for insuring Dolly a home."

"Oh! there's not the shadow of a doubt on that score," said Hester. "He can stay with the Whitbys forever. Indeed, I think they would have been glad enough to secure him for Fanny Whitby, if he would only have waited till the child was older. Fanny is but fifteen. I never dreamed of his falling in love with Dolly."

"But sometimes these great business-houses fail, you know."

"Oh! there are plenty who want him. In fact, he is invaluable as an assistant and translator, and need never be out of business. Besides, he has splendid expectations; and I have seen the letters sent by his lawyers, in which they say he is sure to win his case."

"What case?"

"Hasn't Dolly told you? Why, some of the estates, confiscated in the late war, are to be restored to his family. Oh, yes! I am French scholar enough to translate fairly, and it is very plain that he is to be compensated at the rate of a round million. It seems as if Dolly must be pretty safe in the matter of provision for her future. And then, he certainly is a lovable fellow! As for Dolly, you can see for yourself, she worships him as much as he worships her."

"Yes, and so much the worse if he be proved a scoundrel," I said.

"Why do you talk that way? what have you heard?" asked Hester anxiously.

"Nothing, upon my honor: no one has spoken a word to his disadvantage. On the contrary, everybody speaks in his praise. But I want stronger proof than his mere assertion. I cannot give my sister's happiness in the keeping of a stranger, and that stranger a foreigner, unless I have something more decisive. What about his sister?" I asked.

"Poor fellow! he is very much worried. Since her fall from her horse, she has been confined to her bed; and the last news was, that her life was in danger."

"He seems going to the opera pretty lively for a man whose only sister may be dying," I said.

Hester paused.

"I think this must have been an engagement made some time ago," she said. "Besides, he don't know but she may be out of danger. Why should he spoil Dolly's pleasure?"

"Why, indeed?" and there the matter dropped where it should not. It was on my tongue to speak of the tablet, even to display it to my wife, and set her keen, quick intellect on the scent; but a strange perversity controlled me. I knew it would be safe, a proof of my trust in her, a pleasure to be of any assistance to me; and yet I shrank from taking her into my confidence.

Still, the matter nettled me; and the man, while he attracted, at the same time repelled me. What were all his accomplishments if no truth dwelt on his tongue? How could I trust Dolly to a man who could willingly invent a story to lie and deceive? And that Dolly loved him with all the strength of her young, pure heart, I knew. My doubts angered her: she defended him against all accusations.

"And now I am going over to mother's," said Hester, rising.

I rose too.

"No, Hal: sit down. You seldom have a quiet evening to yourself, and Jenkins is doing nothing but nodding at the kitchen-fire. I will take him."

"But really, don't you care?" I queried.

"Not a bit. You can't probably see mother; very likely Miriam is with her, and wouldn't go down-stairs; and you'd have nobody to talk to. So sit down, and be a good boy till I come back."

She looked laughingly over her shoulder at me as she started for her wraps; and presently she came to kiss me good-by, fully equipped.

"There goes that horrible bell again! Why won't they let you have a little peace of your life! It does seem as if your evenings ought to belong to you!" Hester exclaimed.

Jenkins opened the door, ushering in a young lady, dressed in the height of fashion. Her bold, bright black eyes sparkled at sight of me.

"Well! it is really delightful to find *one* clergyman at home!" she said, with a lovely smile, that displayed fine, even white teeth.

"Pray be seated, miss," I said. "Hester, I will see you to the door, and call for you in half an hour."

I went out with my wife.

"Hal," she whispered, "I never saw such an impudent face in my life! Beware of her."

"I promise she shall not carry me off bodily," was my reply, laughing.

"Oh! I'm not afraid of that; she don't want *you*; she's after your pocket-book," Hester said.

"I didn't count upon it, but perhaps you might as well come for me;" and she was gone.

I went back to my strange visitor.

"Ah! this looks so like my own old home," she said, as I found her comfortably seated opposite the fire. "My poor papa was a clergyman. You have heard of Dean McKatheron?"

"Indeed I have! Was he your father?" I asked.

"Yes; he died five years ago: and the Rev. Mr. McKatheron, rector of All Souls, is my own cousin. I went to his house at first, but found him away with his family."

I knew that the Rev. Mr. McKatheron had gone abroad. Never stopped to wonder why she had not been made aware of his absence.

"And then I called on the rector of the Ascension, but he and his wife had gone to visit a parishioner out of town. Oh, dear! and I was *so* tired! Do you believe, I went the rounds of all the clergymen before I came here? I never dreamed I should find you at home."

She took a dainty lace kerchief out of her reticule, and a subtle odor was wafted through the room. I am very sensitive in the matter of perfumes, but this fragrance seemed a part of her aristocratic presence.

"Oh! I suppose I must tell you my story," she continued. "It is so stupid — well, so commonplace, to have a story to tell! but really, I think you will pardon me. I came here, not intending to stay more than a few days, and only brought a hundred dollars with me. How I lost the money, whether it was taken out of my pocket, or I left it in the car, I am totally unable to tell. I think, however, my pocket was picked; for, when I went to pay the coachman, my purse was gone. It's very humiliating to have to go to a hotel without money; so I hurried to my cousin's house, to find it shut up. I thought if I could borrow fifty dollars, or even twenty, to pay my hotel-bills and my fare back — I don't know what I shall do if I can't."

She crossed her delicately kidded hands on her knees. The firelight brought out the curves and tints of a very beautiful face; but the small red lips began to tremble, and I saw the tears gather in her eyes.

"You will have to stay at the hotel to-night, I suppose," I said.

"Oh, yes! and I forgot to say that I can leave security," she added, suddenly starting from her pose of deep dejection. "I have my diamond ring with me, — the last gift of my dear father. I should insist upon leaving it."

"No, indeed! If I had the money," I faltered, having before me the memory of the score of times I had been made the victim of mercenary callers, "you should have it in a moment. But I think"— I took a small roll of bills from my pocket. It amounted to just nine dollars and fifty cents.

"I really don't know," I said, pondering the matter as I held the money in my hands. "I"—

"O sir!" and the small figure drew up, while a proud gesture and a sad, resigned expression stole over the perfect face. "I see that you doubt me, sir, and I cannot bear that. Keep your money, sir, for what you may consider a worthier object. I do not ask charity: I simply wanted a *loan!* Pray excuse me for this intrusion. I will go elsewhere. I could not *allow* you to assist me now."

That settled it. If the reader should happen to be a man, and had been in my place, it would have settled him. If Hester had been there, she would have screwed her courage up, and — let her go.

"I beg you will allow me to loan you this," I said. "I only hesitated as the sum was to be applied to a particular object, but I shall make it up immediately. Pray, miss, oblige me by borrowing this trifling sum. I only wish it were more."

My beautiful visitor flushed, hesitated, bit her lip, and, after a pretty bit of hesitancy, condescended to retract. She looked at the money, and gently drew off her glove. A diamond solitaire sparkled on one of her slender fingers.

"Indeed, I cannot consent to this," I said, as she held it out.

"And I will not take the money without leaving my pledge," she answered, with her very bright smile. "So there it is."

Absolutely, I never felt so mean in my life. Here was the daughter of a prominent clergyman, whose death had been so sincerely mourned, leaving his gift with me as if I had been a pawnbroker. But what could I do? She persisted, until at last I was forced to relent.

"Oh, you can't realize how good you have been to me!" she said, with her beaming smile. "Think if I had gone to a hotel, how terrible it would have been to be denied admission! And, of course, they don't know me; and cousin John, my only living relative in the city, not here to testify for me. I really do not know how to thank you."

She bowed herself out of the room with an exquisite air of refinement, leaving the vision of a perfect face in sunshine and in shade, to haunt me.

"Had I been wise, or foolish?"

Hester came home just as I was about to start for her.

"Poor mamma was asleep, so I did not stay," she said. "Now, what of your visitor? She certainly was pretty, but dreadfully brazen. What did you give her?"

"I gave her nothing, my dear."

"Oh! I am glad you are beginning to find"—

"But I *lent* her a small sum," and I felt my cheeks burn. "It was ridiculously small for the equivalent she would insist upon my taking. See this!"

"Oh! a diamond!" exclaimed my wife.

She took it. I grew in stature and wisdom at once. She carried it under the light — turned it round — smiled.

"Well, madam, what do you think now?" I asked triumphantly.

"I think you are an awful goose!" said Hester, bursting into a laugh, "a dear, old, soft-hearted goose! But then, how could you know? Now, you have often laughed at what you call my instinct. Why, Hal, dear, she wouldn't have *dared* to give that ring into my fingers. See here: it never cost fifty cents. Diamond! ha, ha! it's a miserable piece of glass, though prettily cut. Well, you *have* been duped! You'll never see her again."

I told her the whole story.

"If I had been here," she said, "that minx would have gone as empty-handed as she came.

I know my heart isn't as big as yours, but I've got an awful bump of incredulity."

Later I found that Hester's decision was correct. Out of the twenty clergymen in the city, fifteen or sixteen had been duped by this bogus daughter of a royal line.

"She enlisted my sympathies at once," said the Rev. Doctor Cutler, a Methodist minister, "by presenting herself as the niece of our late lamented bishop. I lent her twenty dollars; and she left with me a valuable agate ring, she said, and which, I suppose, is no more an agate than yours is a diamond. She will probably get out of the city in some disguise, and so evade justice. No man should allow himself to be taken by surprise; but we clergymen, as a rule, are shamefully easy to dupe. But then, what can one do? Must we steel our hearts to every tale of suffering, or rate our charities according to the personal charms of the recipients? I confess I don't know how to solve the problem."

Neither do I.

CHAPTER XIX.

*"And in her eyes was something strange,
A look as of another world."*

THE warm June days had come, with glowing sunshine and tender shadow. The peach-trees in the rectory-yard were all abloom with that fresh pink tinge that one sees only in the heart of a living conch shell, and that trembles, now into fainter, now into deeper, beauty, as the outer light encircles it.

My cares seemed to accumulate as the warm weather approached. The professor's wife, now a helpless invalid, required the presence of Hester so often, that it was useless to think of taking the customary vacation. My special and particular bore, Mrs. Dickory, found it convenient to make a great many calls. She had lately become the mother of the eighth, as she proudly called her last achievement in maternity, and was correspondingly communicative and confidential as to her family affairs. If the paternal head of the house of Dickory volunteered advice after the manner of tyrannical husbands inclined to take a drop too much, she came to me with the grievance. Her utter indifference to my intimations that my time was too valuable to be taken up with such trivialities, broadened the comedy of her confessions, until, when I saw the flaming red or yellow or green of her much ornamented head-gear, I involuntarily took up either a book or my pen, and let her gabble on, if I could not escape in time through the back door.

"I'm goin' to bring my Dolce for baptiserm nex' sabbath," she said one day: "but she's an awful one to hold, an' she hates water like pizen; so if you'd please be kerful 'n not let the drops run over her nose, — which is her sensitivest part, being as she has had a cold ever sence being born, — it will keep her more quieter."

"What did you say the name was?" I asked, forgetting myself, and looking up from my book.

"Dolce. Dickory called me a heathen: he hain't got no imagination, nor what I call fine feelin's. Fer a man as has lived with *me* now goin' on fifteen years, — well, I were married at fourteen, so I'm not in my thirties yet, — I must say he is as destitute of idolatry as if he had been in daily companionship with a woman as thinks scrubbing is her only vocation, and what she were born to. You mightn't think it, but I *hev* writ poetry; and, if my fambly was smaller, I should contribute occasionally, I don't doubt."

"But where did you get the name?" I asked, much amused. Her husband's *idolatry*, which she supposed to mean ideality, corresponded so aptly to the terrible name she intended to fasten on her helpless offspring, that it fixed itself in my memory as a standing anecdote.

"Why, I've seen it in singing-books like this, and in books of stories:" she handed me a slip of paper, on which was written in a coarse hand, "*Dolce far niente.*"

"It kinder took my fancy," she said, "and I do like originality:" this word she pronounced with the *g* hard. "Only, I thought I would change it a little, and call her Dolce Fanny Niente: the whole name kinder sounds so foreign-like, and I'm tired of the usual stock."

"My good woman, that's no name at all," I said: "it is merely suggestive of a person too lazy to keep awake. You wouldn't subject your child to such a burden. Everybody would laugh. Call her Fanny, or Dora, or something understandable, or else I can't baptize your child."

"Then, I've got to give in to Dickory," she said, looking meditative; "and it's what I've never did yet. But I know how to git over that

—*you* shall give it a name, and I'll be honored and evermore obliged."

"No, no: I would not take the responsibility," I said hastily. "Choose between you"—

"I think you said Fanny or Dora," she responded complacently. "Don't you see you've already done it? I'll call her Fanny, and much obliged, I'm sure."

"You may call her Methuselah, for all I care," I said, feeling my long-suffering patience oozing out at my finger's-ends, as I rose. "I've got an appointment, and you must excuse me."

"Them pants is reely going at the knees: how beautifully Dickory could fit you!" was the quiet rejoinder, with a good-natured smile. Then she took a hair-pin out of her back hair, and fastened a straggling lock on her forehead, looked in my glass with a perfectly complacent face, while I stood quivering with anger, with my hand on the back of my chair, adjusted her cotton gloves, looked herself all over admiringly, wished me good-morning, and walked out of the study with the air of an empress.

The woman's vanity was astonishing, nay, it reached the point of sublimity, as she regally turned, came back, and asked for a drink of water, and languishingly drank it, looking at me. Then with a soft sigh, and a tragic shake of the head, as if she were the victim of untold sorrows, she departed.

On such occasions I despised myself heartily for the restraint I was forced to put upon my temper. Clergyman as I was, it would have been an immense satisfaction if I could have taken her by the shoulders, and put her bodily out of the place, with an injunction to her to go, and come no more. But what could I do? she was a member of my church, in good standing.

What could I do with such people as the Eddys, who were starving themselves, and wronging their poor, crippled boy by denying him the education he craved, and the art-surroundings, the outside education of the senses coming from things graceful and beautiful to the eye? — so craving them that it was pitiful to see the bare walls, all cracked and crumbling, ornamented with such pictures as the poor lad could find in odd numbers of papers and magazines, coarse daubs colored by home-made pigments, and now and then a bit of china suggestive of costlier *bric-à-brac*. They also were members of the church; and, say what you will, such personal idiosyncrasies are seldom touched by the pulpit. Ay, be plain as you dare be, even to the verge of naming and pointing out the culprits, and they will meet you with the sweetest, most debonair smiles, and thank you for your "splendid sermon!"

What good did all my preaching do Tom Tracy? His impertinently beautiful face never moved a muscle. Did he believe I meant him? God knows. There were two or three other somewhat public targets in the congregation — a hundred for all I could tell. Perhaps my shots were meant for them. At all events, the men I did mean them for never flinched. Did I not know, that before me sat, Sunday after Sunday, rich men who rejoiced in their riches, who surrounded themselves with their panoply of wealth, and never gave to the poor, seldom to missions, and only now and then to some popular charity, that their names might be sounded abroad? Was I not fully conscious, as in the case of Tom Tracy, that gossip told strange stories concerning this and that dignitary, and that gossip had the truth to fall back upon? Was it a pleasant fact for me to be well aware that some of my members, conspicuous for active work in the church, owned places so disreputable that it were a sin to name, and gathered in their heavy rents from such foul sources to throw into the Lord's treasury? Did I tell my wife that I was going to write thus broadly concerning my colleagues? No — or this book perhaps had not been written.

As it is, I have said what I have, to prove how hard it is for the most painstaking, ay, or the most eloquent, of God's messengers, to correct an error, or convict the human heart of evil. What good may be done eventually,— what phase of existence may be reached, in which the sleepy soul may arouse and remember, and perhaps reform,— who can tell? I do not detract from my calling. It is glorious; and, if the reward comes not till hereafter, it is all we have, or ought to have, a right to expect.

I seldom saw Miriam, even at the house of my wife's mother. Hester was overflowing with admiration for her: her executive ability, her fitness for the sick-room, her tenderness, of these she was always talking. Marguerite was now almost installed in the rectory. Beautiful as she was, and winning in a high degree, there was something repulsive to me about the child. Her habitual reference to her dead mother annoyed me. I could not reason her out of the hallucination that she saw her almost constantly, talked with, was advised by her. The delicate dignity with which the child refuted my reasoning, sometimes awed me; and the interpretation that she put upon my explanations was often beyond her years, and gave her a weird kind of pre-eminence over other children of her age, by whom I was surrounded.

I shall never forget one starry night when her prescience was something startling and wonderful, but which I attribute to an extraordinary gift of sympathy, with perhaps the aid of a clairvoyant quality of the mind.

Dolly had gone to a concert with Ravaillac. Hester was lying on the sofa after a visit to her mother, whom she had left much better, every way, than she had been for weeks.

"Now I'm going to nurse myself a little," she said. "I have a fearful headache. Come, Marguerite, lay your cool little fingers on my forehead: you always help me."

The child was reading in a collection of stories which I had bought for her the Christmas before; but she left her book at once, and seated herself beside Hester. I remember how uneasy I felt, a trifle jealous perhaps, that of late she seemed to have taken my place; but Hester brightened at once, and became communicative.

"I had a letter from Marie Tracy that was," she said, after a few moments; "and I judge she is very happy. She is in Florence, she and her husband, or were when she wrote; and one would think her an old Florentine, from the way she mentions all the grand old places I remember so well,—Ponte Vecchio, San Martino, San Marco, the Porte Romana, and the Trinita. It seems but yesterday that we were there; and, if you had only been with me, my happiness would have been complete," she adds, looking over at me with beaming eyes.

I smile; but my glance is arrested by Marguerite, who seems looking at the clock, and yet beyond it. What is it that makes the large dark eyes dilate and deepen, and the whole exquisite face, delicate as a star, perfect as a dream of paradise, glow with a rapt, inspired expression?

The child turns, and glances at me, and I am chilled to the heart: I cannot tell why. If I could escape from her, I would. I bethink me of some unfinished work in the study; and, begging Hester to excuse me for a few moments, I retire thither.

Jenkins confronts me, combing his long hair with his fingers by the fire. I am glad he is there, for the gas is out.

"I was just going to shut up," he says. Jenkins always speaks as if my study were a shop. He lights the gas, and goes out. I want him to stay, but am ashamed to say so; and I sit down to my neglected correspondence, much like a culprit whose sin is ever before him. But I find I cannot write. Something oppresses me — something stays cold at my heart. I look round on the old familiar backs of my books. Here is a treatise on philosophy, three centuries old. My father bought it in London at a great book-sale. It is filled with curious plates, some of which I seem to see through the covers. They are not all pleasant pictures, nor graven in the highest style of art.

Presently there is a knock at the door. I shiver as Marguerite presents herself, a luminous picture, apparently evolved out of the darkness. Before the door is shut, I catch sight of a cluster of stars.

"I didn't like to tell cousin Hester," the child — child or demon ? — says, leaning on the wide arm of my chair, and looking into my face, while I shiver at her near proximity.

"Why, what have you to tell?" I ask sharply, conscious of my injustice in harboring such feelings.

"Aunt Harriette is dead!"

A breath from the unseen seemed touching my cheek as she spoke.

I started from my chair.

"What do you mean?" I asked sharply, so sharply that she fell back a few paces from me, and looked grieved.

"But, my dear, you know it *must* be nonsense," I said, with an attempt at kindness. "Hester was there less than an hour ago, and she brought back the news that Mrs. Vaughan was better than she had been for a long time."

"I know it; but I saw mamma, and she told me."

I clinched my hands, the feeling of anger came over me so suddenly.

"I have told you a thousand times that you were mistaken"—

Some one knocked at the door. I opened it. John, the professor's man-of-all-work, stood there.

I knew what he would say before he opened his lips, but I fought against the conviction. That steadfast gaze of Marguerite had explained it all, unwilling as I should have been to confess it.

"Well, what is it, John?" The great, dusky vault of heaven glittering with its countless stars seemed so near that I might have touched it with my hand.

"It's bad news, sir. Professor says you must break it to Miss Hester. The madam died sitting up, 'fore they could git her into bed, about half an hour ago. It just fell like a thunder-clap, it was so onlooked for."

Marguerite glided back into the house. She had heard all he said, and did not even cast back at me one glance of triumph.

"What is it?" cried Hester, as John and I went in together.

I took her outstretched hands, and kissed her on the forehead.

"It is bad news, dear. Be strong, Hester—I can help you bear it."

"Is it — mother?" she asked faintly: "is she dying?"

No one answered. The silence was appalling. Hester sank into her chair, trembling, still holding my hand convulsively. The light and color had all gone out of her face, but she was very calm.

CHAPTER XX.

*"Oh country sights and country sounds!
Oh childhood's days forever gone,
When life was one unbroken joy!"*

HESTER mourned for her mother, and spent much of her time with the professor, to whom her presence seemed for some days almost indispensable. There had never been a complete sympathy between my wife and Mrs. Vaughan. In fact, the former had somewhat disappointed her mother. Hester was what she called strong-minded, and vigorously asserted the rights of her sex. And, furthermore, Mrs. Vaughan had visited very little at our house, never having quite forgiven Hester for refusing so many brilliant offers, to settle down at last as only the wife of a clergyman who worked for his living in a quiet, humdrum way.

Hester went into deep mourning, very much against my wishes, for I have an utter abhorence of the fashion of crape; and presently came the changes that we knew would inevitably come.

The professor wished to break up house-keeping. He offered his house to rent, admirably furnished as it was, he to keep a suite of rooms including his library, and board with the incoming family, — a physician, it proved to be, with a large practice and no children.

"That throws Miriam out," Hester said, as we talked it over. "Papa is willing to provide for her, or to find her a situation; but Miriam is so delicate, I hate to let her go among strangers. Besides, I shall never forget her kindness to poor mamma."

"And Marguerite," I said.

"Yes, Marguerite," said Hester, after a thoughtful pause. "I don't think papa ever cared much about her: it was a whim of mamma's to take her, and now the child is breaking her heart because it is proposed to send her back to England. Either that or a boarding-school, papa says. I certainly am very much attached to the child, and she is not constitutionally fitted to live among strangers. My dear, I have a plan: if only you will second it!" she looked up anxiously at me, the color flitting back and forth in her cheeks. I would do any thing for her, and she knew it; knew that just now she stood on a plane beyond all the ideals of womanhood that I had ever imagined; knew that her will was my law, and that, for the sake of the joy to come, I would unhesitatingly have sacrificed my most cherished plans, that nothing should interfere with her happiness.

"Then, why cannot Miriam and Marguerite come right here? Dolly is away much of her time, or writing in her room; and I don't want to be lonesome now. Marguerite is progressing delightfully in her studies, and pupil and teacher are very much attached to each other. It can make no difference with you. Then," she added eagerly, "we can leave for our vacation with the comfortable feeling that there is somebody in the house."

Had a bomb exploded at my feet, I could not have been more completely taken by surprise. I had supposed that the professor would provide for the future of Miriam, and send the child Marguerite to boarding-school. Both teacher and child were distasteful to me. To have them in the house at all times and seasons, to experience that indefinable something in the presence of Miriam, that was completely antagonistic to my nature, and yet to feel that she exercised a subtle spell, that was by no means a pleasant one, over my consciousness, made the proposition for a moment seem too monstrous to reflect upon with any degree of calmness. There was a certain insincerity in Miriam that made me feel painfully that she could not be counted upon in any crisis — that for the sake of excusing herself she could accuse another. Of course, I did not know exactly how she felt toward me, only there was the conviction that she cherished something approaching revenge; that she would be a constant thorn in my side, and enjoy seeing me miserable. Besides, it was possible that I should be thrown very much in her society as Hester's health became more markedly delicate, and I dreaded that. There was the refuge of the church-study, to be sure; but I was no monk, and craved sympathy and association. All these thoughts shot through my mind, quickened by the consciousness that I might have made every thing clear if I had only told Hester that little episode, would only tell her now. But time upon that subject had only tied my tongue the tighter.

"I hope you're not going to object," said Hester. I had noticed that of late she was more easily irritated than in her normal state of perfect health, and I carefully avoided every cause that might subject her to nervous moods or unhappy intervals.

"I want to think of it, dear," I said at last, reluctantly. "Of course, being your wish gives it great weight with me; but — are you sure you will like Miriam as well, as a constant associate? In some cases, even where there is a near relationship, distance lends enchantment to the view, and" —

"Why, Hal, dear! how unjust to dear Miriam!" said Hester with some vehemence. "You have no idea what a lovely character hers is — nothing mean, sordid, or selfish about her. I shall never forget her devotion, both to my mother and her own. And she is so sweet and companionable, she can take my place in so many things. I am not going to be selfish, and let you pine in loneliness because I can't be always with you. Why, dear, it's *more* for your sake than my own that I want Miriam!"

The dear, unselfish little woman! How immeasurably superior to all the women I had ever known, did she seem to me then. I clasped her to my bosom, declaring that I would rather share her solitude, even her hours of pain and imprisonment, rather than spend moments in any other companionship.

"Perhaps Miriam will not care to come," I said. "Have you spoken to her about it?"

"Oh, yes! and she was only afraid that fortune held no such good thing in store for her. Now you must be a good boy, and submit. I have arranged for a sort of half nursery, half study, for Marguerite; and the child is so pleased! She loves us both dearly, Hal, and I couldn't consent to send her among strangers. Dolly is pleased too;—and Dolly will probably soon leave us for good. Has Ravaillac spoken to you yet?"

"Not yet," I said, with misgivings. I felt an unaccountable sadness steal over me. My home, which had hitherto been so sacred, a source of joy, pure, ecstatic, and holy, was soon to be a divided place. I felt, by some strange law of the heart, as yet unread by nature, unknown to science, that, the moment Miriam stepped over our threshold, my peace and the peace of my beloved Hester would be threatened, if not sacrificed. It was as if I could see that Miriam had been biding her time.

At length I acquiesced with the best grace I could; and Miriam came one sunny day, and all her trunks and belongings with her. Hester had given one of the best rooms for her occupancy, and seemed quite overjoyed that now her household was completed.

"I made papa promise that he would come every Sunday to dinner," she said, beaming upon me. "It will make him feel so much less lonesome!"

Lonesome! there was but little danger of being lonesome now, in any part of the house. Marguerite took music-lessons, Miriam practised indefatigably, and I soon began to sigh for the old quiet. Hester had prepared a pretty little apartment, leading out of the nursery, for her own sewing-room; and there I spent much of my time, though Hester assured me that it was her especial domain, and she should only allow my visits till I got accustomed to the change.

We spent our vacation with my sisters; and, while there, Belle was quietly married. My wife enjoyed the beautiful country-haunts with the enthusiasm of a child.

"I wonder you were not all poets," she said, as we went from point to point, where as a boy I had studied and fished, and gone berry-picking. "Every view is more beautiful than the last, and I never saw such trees!" Then the thimbleberry bushes, the great tracts of wild strawberry and blackberry vines, the sun-lighted rivers, the natural arches made by bended branches over the long green forest aisles, the blue thread of a rivulet, the gorgeous sunsets — never was there a more delighted recipient of country hospitality.

Oh, could I have staid there eternally with my wife, amid those rustic sights and sounds! Could we have wandered from day to day, like two happy children, unhindered by contact with the Dickories; the rich vulgar, and the poor proud; the selfish, who deemed themselves prodigies of charity; the stingy generous, and the malevolent urbane; the pews that paid and were arrogant, the pews that did not pay and were impertinent. But God only lets us live in paradise a little at a time, in this world; and that two months of solid enjoyment was all I could have been spared in the dusty record of time. Did I preach? Not once. My brothers in the ministry courteously invited, my sisters implored, and my friends importuned. I wanted to let my other life severely alone, and go back to the old days when the preaching, if not the preacher (who was my own father), was a bore to me. I wonder if that is why I pity the children so in crowded churches, with their vacuous faces and ill-concealed yawns.

At last it was over; at last only the dream was left, to think of once in a while; and I went back refreshed to my sterner duties.

Dolly had been with us, and, once a week, Mr. Ravaillac. It was curious to see how, in his presence, the antipathies of my family took wing. I knew why,—it was the man's consummate tact. It amounted to genius. If Dora looked for a chair, there was he with the most comfortable of rockers, and a smile that would have melted the frozen lips of marble into its counterpart. If one of them lost her spectacles, it was always Mr. Ravaillac who restored them, returning them with so courtly a grace, that the recipient found herself longing to lose them again. To spring forward with a shawl, to move a hassock, roll a table, offer a basket, insist upon precedent, and all the time to make it apparent, by little, unobtrusive services, that Dolly was the light of his eyes, the very pulse of his heart! Opposition halted, prejudice vanished. He could say, "I came, I saw, I conquered!"

"I believe I could live forever in the atmosphere of Mount Myrtle," Hester would often say, busy over her basket of little things. "We will come here every summer, Hal."

We found the house on our return much the same as we left it, only the carpets had been shaken, and every thing put straight.

"Miriam is such a good housekeeper!" Hester said: "you will not find any difference when I am not down-stairs."

Did I not? It would be hard for me to tell how I found it something less than home, but I did.

Miriam had grown more beautiful, and paid more attention to dress than formerly. Gradually I saw that a change came over her. From demure, sad self-possession, she became bright and attentive. It seemed sometimes as if Hester had delegated her own social duties to her cousin. She brought me my dressing-gown, and warmed my slippers. At Hester's earnest entreaty, I took her with me now and then to lectures, to concerts.

"You must make poor, lonely Miriam as happy as you can," Hester would say. "Sometimes it seems to me that you do not like her. She feels it too."

"Why, what has she ever said?" I asked in some alarm.

"Nothing, not a word. I wish some good man would come along whom she could love; for of course she is dependent now, and she feels it: perhaps that is what I meant when I said she thinks you do not like her. Of course, like all young girls, Miriam would be happier with a lover of her own."

"Then, why don't she get one?" I asked bluntly.

"She is not one of the pushing kind," said Hester simply; "so you must be very good to her."

CHAPTER XXI.

*"And all her words were bitter,
And all her glances flame."*

I WAS sitting in my study one evening, admiring the effect of some statuettes I had been beguiled by an itinerant Italian into purchasing, when Jenkins thrust his long ears in at the door.

"Sure, it's Mr. Ravaillac as wishes to see you," he said, and stepped aside.

The Frenchman entered, paused on the threshold, gave me a penetrating look, and then stood like a prince, if princes ever await the pleasure of their hosts.

"Won't you be seated, sir?" I said, and pointed to a vacant chair.

He flushed, bowed, and slid with easy grace into the chair indicated, crossed one leg over the other, rested the hand which held his hat on that, and so, his handsome face somewhat troubled, proceeded to tell me his story. It was very modestly told. He had loved Dolly from the first moment of seeing her: he loved her — and his look grew rapturous — as no man ever loves a woman twice. He would ask permission to show me some of his papers: he had one from the American consul in Paris, from the French minister in Washington. He had that very day heard good news: his case was gained; the home of his ancestors restored, though not their rank. That was impossible as yet, while France remained republican. His *grand-mère* had cabled the news over her own name, so had his sister. He held out the two messages. Now he was independent: now he could take his bride to his ancient home. He knew he was asking of me a great prize: but he would swear eternal fidelity, his wife should be to him as a princess of the blood royal, while we should be his ever beloved American kindred; and so he went on, while I listened quietly.

"You ask a great deal, monsieur," I said: "you take my twin sister, my twin soul, some thousands of miles from our home. She has there no friends, no brothers, no sisters, — no one but you. It is a serious question: it may involve serious results. What does Dolly herself say?"

"Ah!" his eyes flashed fire; he crossed his arms upon his breast, while another flood of rapture brightened his face: "she says she will go with me to the ends of the earth."

"And these are your papers?" I asked, as I put my hand upon the package he had placed on the desk. "They are all in French, but the one from the American consul. I cannot read French."

"Ah! but you can easily get it translated." I smiled at his quaint pronunciation. "I myself could translate for you."

"I see," I said, putting my left hand in my waistcoat inner pocket, and suddenly displaying the tablet; "and what is this?"

That the man was not habitually a deceiver was proved by the quick, deathly pallor that overspread his face, and the start so full of astonishment, and equally marked with guilt. He gasped, and bit his lip. For once his courtliness deserted him, for a rolling "Sacre-e!" issued from his lips.

"You know these, then? don't attempt to deny it. *I* have known for a long time."

He stared at me wildly, threw one hand to his head, and staggered like a drunken man. I thought he would fall.

"I — I am not — prepared" —

"Confess that you are an impostor!" I thundered; "that you have sought my sister's hand under false pretences; that you have no sister, no grandmother, no standing, no estates!"

"*Non! non!* my God, *non!*" he cried, taken aback by my vehemence. "I have a sister — a *grand-mère* — a home. — I will not be what you call brow-beaten — *non!* You shall not so address me!"

"You have deceived me — us all," I said sternly. "I read it in your countenance."

"Ah! in a little way — perhaps — in a small way — that is all it seems to us Frenchmen, I swear to you!"

"Don't swear to me. I want none of your protestations: I want the truth. You invented your sister — made her sick or well at your caprice: you invented her husband, — the colonel of the French army. You see that I have information gained from a private source. You are a liar, sir! and you cannot have my sister."

For one moment I stood on the defensive, for his straight figure swayed and trembled with sudden anger. I thought he would strike me. But no: he preserved his dignity, simply saying, "You are *her* brother! — I cannot touch you."

There was sincerity in this, grace, magnanimity. His voice had the ring of manliness, his eyes the look of truth. A moment more, and Dolly stood in our midst, so purely beautiful under the fleecy ornaments on shoulders and head, that she seemed like an angel just come from heaven.

"Brother, what is this? are you angry?" she asked.

"What has happened? Your voice came through to the parlor. Ernest," she added, turning to Ravaillac, "what is it?"

"It is this," I said, fixing Ravaillac with my eyes. "This man who has the audacity to ask for your hand, is a vile impostor. He came to you with lies on his lips, and in your pure presence he dares not deny it."

"Oh! he must, he will deny it!" she said, in a low, passionate voice.

Another moment he was on his knees at her feet, his head buried in her garments. Then he looked up. Death seemed to be stamped in his face. She was gazing down at him like a pitying spirit. He was shaking from head to foot.

"It was a sudden temptation — and — I was overcome — but I will tell you — I will tell you" — and a terrible sob shook him from head to foot.

"I will not have you kneel, Ernest. Get up," said Dolly, with sudden sternness. All the color had left her face. She gathered her garments, and held them back as if fearing contamination from his touch. He saw the gesture, quickly caught at them again, and kissed the hem of her dress with passionate earnestness.

Then, as she drew back again, he let them fall, rose to his feet, half turned away, and leaned over the back of his chair.

For a few seconds there was utter silence. Then she went towards him, very grave, offered her little white hand, and as he took it, with a renewal of hope kindling all over his face, and glowing in his eyes, she said, —

"If you have deceived me, Ernest, if you have lied, as my brother says, — my dear, good brother, who has loved me all my life, — good-by. Some other time I may listen to you as a friend; but now — I can't stay here," she added; and with a cry that went to my heart, she hurried out as she had come in, looking like to faint.

"My God! and I was so happy!" he said. "I will nôt live longer! I want not life, nor fortune, nor love without her."

"If you can tell me the truth," I said —

He knelt humbly at my side, nor would he listen to my commands that he should rise. He talked rapidly: every sentence seemed to burn with truth.

"I am not noble — that is all. My father was a soldier. My grandfather was with Napoleon at Austerlitz. He won a medal for bravery. My father died, my mother died: they were poor, but I was adopted by a merchant and his wife. My sister was taken by another family. I was the same as son to the good people. They cared for my *grand-mère* because her husband had distinguished himself. These good people lost all in the war: they were made poor, but not before they had educated me. I was all they had: they loved me, and I adored them. Yes, yes, I have a sister — *mon ange — petite* Elise. I swear to you she is no myth, but flesh of my flesh, bone of my bone. She is also married, and has a little son; but her husband is only a plain man, no officer of the French army. That is only where I sinned — yes, I own it with shame, with very much shame! — I wanted to seem better than I am. For her sake I wanted to be a noble, unfortunate through injustice. Now you have the truth. God has helped you more than men have helped me. But I will tell you, and you shall believe! — those to whom I belong are honest, honorable people; and I could curse myself that I was ashamed of their humble position — they who did so much for me. It was unmanly: I see it now. I am unworthy to take the hand of a good man; and, alas! I have lost the esteem of the woman I worship. Here are my letters. Take them where you will: the truth shall be proved. Here is the paper that gives evidence that my kind foster-parents have returned to them the wealth they earned in business, that was taken from them during the war. I despise myself that I was ashamed of them. I kneel here at your feet, and ask, implore, your forgiveness. Do not condemn me for my weakness. Have a little patience with me. I cannot live and endure your contempt. Tell me that you do not think me wholly unworthy."

What could I do? his qualifications socially were simply immense. I found that in my heart I loved the fellow, and also found my sympathy taking the shape of pity for his misfortunes rather than his sin. And yet I could say to him, —

"Sir, I despise a liar."

"Yes," he said humbly, rising from his knees: "I confess I have forfeited the good opinion of honest men and women. Good-by, sir: you shall no more see me."

There was a look in his large dark eyes that moved me more than any word he had spoken.

"And what of Dolly?" I said sternly.

He shook his head: his lip trembled. With a gesture indescribable, he said, —

"It was paradise — and I have lost it. But what can I say more? Of what good is it to me? I care not for life: it is over, it is done for me." His hand was on the door-knob.

"We will not part in anger," I said after a

pause; and I stood up, my heart aching for my sister. "What Dolly may do in the future, I can't say. She, too, shares in my hatred for a — for deception," I added hastily. "But it is my duty as a minister of God to comfort and forgive. You are penitent — God help you and console you."

I held out my hand. He took it with a heavy, suppressed sob, in both his, carried it to his lips, then went out into the dark. I looked at my hand half reverently, standing there alone: a large tear had plashed down upon it. I took my handkerchief, and wiped it softly out.

As I expected, Dolly was not to be seen on my return. Miriam sat by the centre-table by herself. She looked up, smiling.

"Where's Hester?" I asked.

"Hester went up-stairs early, with a bad headache. Dolly came in a few minutes ago, and she, too, rushed up-stairs. Marguerite fell asleep — so you see I have had a sociable evening of it. Mr. Ravaillac promised to come back, and play backgammon with me, but he didn't; and I wanted a game so much! See, the table is set: won't you play with me?"

I was not in the mood for games of any kind: my mind was occupied with the exciting scene that had so recently occurred. Miriam had the penetration to discover that something unpleasant had jarred upon my feelings. In another moment my great, comfortable arm-chair was drawn forward, the lamp-shade turned, so that the light should not strike my eyes, and the backgammon-table moved aside. Of course, I acknowledged the courtesy by seating myself in the cosey, softly illuminated room; and not long after that we two were playing backgammon. I can recall the scene, — the shadowy sides of the room; an ornament here, half in shadow; a book-case there; a bit of gilding; a touch of color; and Miriam, her soul in her face, watching my moves intently.

We had had three games, two of which were won by her, and were nearly through the third, when I observed her hand trembled. I looked up: her eyes were swimming in moisture, and singularly lustrous. Before I could speak, she had burst into a violent passion of tears, sobbing and weeping as if her heart would break.

Startled, astonished, and at last a little angry, I sat back in my chair, and looked at the girl.

"Miriam, what does this mean?" at last I forced myself to say, trying to speak with sternness, but I fear failing.

"Oh! don't speak to me! don't look at me!" she cried, drawing in her breath like one in pain. "There are so — so many things — to — make one miserable. I am so unhappy! so wretched."

My impulse was to leave the room at once; but a touch of human nature, perhaps of curiosity, held me passive.

"I am sure Hester thought she was doing her best by you," I said.

I think she set her teeth hard together.

"Hester!" she said, and the tone made me pitiless. "It was always Hester!— Hester always came between me and happiness."

"Then, if the trouble is with you and Hester, you must fight it out between yourselves," I said, as I rose from my chair.

"Do you think I would say any thing to Hester?" exclaimed the girl, also rising, and dashing the tears away. And then she burst into a torrent of reproaches that fairly stunned me. To whom was she indebted for a life of isolation, a heart starved and broken, but to me? Yes, I could stand there at the sacred desk, and preach to people about their sins, and look and move among my congregation without reproach, while my own record was that of a hypocrite and a deceiver. She held my letters to prove as much — she held *me!* She could fill my home with hatred if she chose, could make Hester despise me! — and there she stood, launching out her thunderbolts with the passion of a Fury, looking, as she did so, like a beautiful fiend.

At last the day of retribution had come.

And I — what could I do? There was no possibility of inflicting punishment: she was a woman, and I had furnished her the weapons with which to strike at my happiness. I stood for a while stunned and helpless.

"After this," I said, when there was a lull in the tempest of words, "it will be no longer possible for you to remain here, Miss Hope."

"And who will put me out? Not you. Hester has my ear, and I have hers. I can wind her round my finger, especially *now*. Oh! I said to myself, I would make you suffer such torment as I have felt; and I will. For a time, *I* shall be mistress here!"

The woman's audacity overpowered me. The grievance was singular, subtle, and sudden. For a few moments, I had that sort of helpless feeling that the bird, perhaps, feels when the eye of the charmer is fastened upon it. How to make Hester aware of the hostile force in our little household? She had perfect faith in Miriam. Towards her the girl was a pattern of all the virtues, a mystic compound of the woman and the angel. She relieved her of care. Her manipulations often banished the headaches that were now so frequent; and the buoyancy of her temperament bridged over those lapses of despondency in which Hester was no longer my sweet and smiling priestess, but foreboded terrible things, and was sure she was going to die.

She had spoken of letters. What letters had she in her possession that could possibly compromise me? I knew I had now and then written her little notes; but I knew, also, that they all ended, "Yours respectfully." That last letter, perhaps, in the excess of my pity, my self-torment, in that I might have said something, which, wrenched out of meaning, might be used for my torture.

It was an unpleasant fact to face, that Miriam cherished even now a fierce passion that touched the borders of hate; and I shrank from it as one shrinks from a deadly danger, and yet knows not how to escape. It was to be my thorn in the flesh, unseen by any other than the eye of God, to go with me wherever I went, to lie down and rise up with me, unless in some way I could rid my home of the incubus that shadowed it, and threatened my domestic happiness. I could not condescend to bandy words with a woman: it would have been a relief could I have put her bodily out of the house, and have done with her.

But her presence was due to the express wishes of my wife; and if any thing could be done, which I doubted then, it must be done through her. At all events, one thing I could do. I would let her severely alone.

How little I reckoned on a woman's strategy!

CHAPTER XXII.

"Shall the fight be never ended?
Shall the conquest ne'er be gained?"

I THINK even Dolly did not miss Ravaillac more than I did. He was one of those blessings one can better appreciate by its absence. At his entrance, care seemed to vanish; and the Graces, in all sorts of amiable and beautiful forms, took up their abode wherever he chose to stay.

The morning after that stormy interview with Miriam, I purposely delayed going below stairs till the breakfast-bell rang. Even then my heart sank within me, and my apprehensions almost made a farce of my devotions.

I went in really leaning on Hester's strength; for she was unusually well and bright, consequently in good spirits.

To my utter astonishment, there was not a trace of the storm, the passion, of the preceding evening. Quivering mouth and trembling hands were firm enough, and equal to all the demands made upon them. One would never have thought, to look at Miriam, freshly attired, undisturbed and beautiful, that a breeze of annoyance had ever ruffled her calm uniformity of demeanor. Towards me she was all smiles and sunshine, while I sat in dumb amaze. Could that strange episode ever have occurred? Was it not a dream of the night, a picture of my excited fancy?

Dolly came from an early walk just as we were sitting down to breakfast, her cheeks scarlet. It pained me to see how soon the rich glow, born of exercise, faded, and the cheeks looked haggard, the eyes restless and hollow. Plainly she had not slept all night. She talked in her old way, but both manner and matter were exaggerated. I knew Dolly so well!

When she fell on my neck afterwards, and, sobbing, told me how much she had loved Ravaillac, and how drearily she missed him, the pain from her heart reached to mine.

"Surely no girl had brighter prospects," she said. We were in the study, and she was sitting on a hassock at my feet. "I often felt that the rich feast spread before me was more than I had a right to expect. Only think! we were going to travel for a year,—one whole year! Now it is all over, and I cannot even respect the man I loved so dearly. That is the hardest of all. If he had only died!" And she bowed her heavy eyes, from which the tears rained, on my knees again.

It was the first time I had had an opportunity to relate to her the story he told in his own vindication. She listened passively, her head on my knee, her face turned from me.

"And in spite of all," I said, "he took my sympathy, my forgiveness, away with him. If he wished it, would you see him again?"

"Never!" she said firmly.

"He is none the worse, you know, for not being nobly born."

"Oh! I didn't mean that — I didn't think of that! What did I, as an American, value in the historic greatness of a title? No: it is his despicable pride in ignoring his humble people, that I cannot forgive. It shows there is something inherently selfish and mean in his character. He wouldn't be safe to trust. I'm afraid of him."

There seemed both common sense and truth in what she said, and yet I found myself in the mood to plead for him.

"I certainly do miss him," I said: "he made our evenings so pleasant!"

"So he did;" and she smiled brightly. "And I noticed, that however wearied I was with the day's labors, or however much I had on my mind, all care fell off in his presence. He certainly had a lovely temperament."

"It would never do for him to come as a friend, then," I ventured.

"No, no: don't think of it — not for him! not for me! No" — and she smiled a little drearily — "we must make the most of Miriam — and Madge." At that the life had gone out of her voice.

"But Miriam and Madge are not — home," I said, somewhat wide of the mark, though the meaning was conveyed.

"No, indeed!" said Dolly sadly. "I never shall feel towards — *her*, as I do for Hester. There is a sense of something hidden about Miriam. I can't describe it exactly, only feel it. It seems as if she were watching one — getting at one's motives, suspecting one. Well, I really ought not to say this — but we are so seldom quite alone now, you and I." Then she looked up at me with wet eyes.

"Hal, had I ought to stay?"

"Dolly! what do you mean?" I asked, in real terror. Hester sick, Miriam mistress — self-constituted — of the rectory, — I could not let her go.

"Since she is here, I feel as if in the way, dear: I do really, and yet I can't say that she ever implies it by word or deed. But I can't help it: I feel so. You know there is the dear old home — and yet " —

"It would kill you, Dolly, to go there and brood, and brood. No: my house is your home. And listen: just now it would not be home without you. For my sake, if you can fight this battle with your heart, here, stay. Lean on me — on a stronger than me, of course; but I will give you my poor help — you know it."

"Yes, I know it." She got up from the hassock, and threw her arms about my neck, kissing me many times, as she had when I was a child; and, while she was thus kissing me, the door opened and shut gently. Somebody looked in. I could not say who, for the face disappeared so instantaneously. I went to the door — nobody was in sight; and I dismissed the matter from my mind, after we had both wondered over it a little.

Then came a time appalling in the annals of that city, — disease that took the form of a plague, and filled many homes with mourning. Of this Hester was kept as much in ignorance as possible, but my continued absences annoyed her. Nervous depression added to her trials a new danger.

She was sure I was not kind to Miriam: not that Miriam complained, but she felt it. I must take Miriam out oftener: her cousin was exhausted by the demands made upon her time and strength. I did not appreciate Miriam's beautiful character. I was sent down-stairs when I would gladly have remained with Hester; and, if I sought relief in my church-study, Hester was unhappy. How did I know that by many a hint; by chance words, carelessly spoken, seemingly; by affecting gayety, while the ready tears were in her eyes, — for this woman could weep at will, — Miriam so wrought on my wife's sensitive mind, that Hester was becoming morbidly anxious on her cousin's account?

There are devilish natures in this world, decided types of the worst forces of our humanity, seeming to lack nothing of the evil side of life, while at the same time they pass for their opposites, the saints. Miriam was one of these, working inch by inch, moving step by step, toward the accomplishment of her purpose. In this case she had fully decided to be revenged on me, for what she supposed was an intentional slight. She had, of course, been vain enough to think she could supplant Hester in my affections, and, failing, chose to believe I had trifled with her. In her soul I think she must have known better.

Meantime I submitted, for Hester's sake, and barely tolerated her cousin. She always managed, however, to go into church when I did, and to wait till I returned, on the pretext of talking to some friend. She sat in the rector's pew; and as she was of a more social temperament than Hester, who was too much given to studying people while talking with them, she made a great many more acquaintances, with whom she conversed wholly about me. The old, foolish gossip was renewed. People looked at each other significantly, and involuntarily smiled whenever I spoke with her.

Unwittingly I overheard something of this on one occasion. I had gone into the large recess, curtained off from my study, to take off my surplice, one day, after a baptismal ceremony. While there, I happened to come across an old book I had long searched for among my collection, but had missed; and, opening it after I had hung up my robe, I stood near the window, reading sentence after sentence on a subject of absorbing interest.

"He's not here," said one of the two ladies who came into the study a moment after. "We'll wait a moment; and, if he don't come, we will go."

Now, it happened that I had special reasons for not wishing to see these people, who were of the same stamp as Mrs. Dickory, only they had been polished — or varnished — in a somewhat higher style. I thought to myself, as I had most entertaining reading, that I would remain quiet, hoping that they would go.

"Queer about that Miss Hope, isn't it?" one of the women questioned, in a low voice.

"Yes: it's often the way when"—and then followed whispering which I could not hear.

"They say it's an old flame of his," said the other.

"Oh, no! it was while the engagement was on with Miss Vaughan. People talked a good deal. I have been told that he gave her a ring, and courted her in right down earnest. People who know her very well, tell me so. It was a blow to her when he married her cousin: I know that. And *now* it's plain to be seen which he likes best. Why, he who runs may read."

I opened the curtain.

"Ladies," I said, "you may say what you will about me, but my wife shall not be insulted." I would have said more; but, with a double cry of dismay, the women fled.

I followed this up on the next Sunday with a sermon on slander, in which I lashed the gossips right and left; but my righteous indignation was probably lost upon those for whom I intended it. Certainly I never had more compliments than for this "most masterly sermon!" I could have taken to my bed in sheer disgust.

"The proper study of mankind is man," the poet says. God help the students, in the pulpit and out!

And yet, there were men and women in that congregation from whose beaming faces I often borrowed my inspiration. They were not of the rich, seldom of the learned. Some of them occupied the seats that were nearest the door, and some of them sat in the free seats. I knew what the grasp of their hands meant: their words outweighed gold to me. I saw upon their careworn brows the imprint of the Father, the peace of the Son. By their humble firesides I tasted ambrosia, and their homely words were as the steps of shining ladders that led up into the light of the glory of the Unseen. They had been "acquainted with grief," like their Master; and the discipline of sorrow had made them saints.

How to be rid of this terrible shadow which darkened my home and threatened my peace? It was a penance for me now to sit in my parlor, to meet Miriam at the table or in Hester's room. She saw with her keen woman's eye that I avoided her, even to rudeness; but she pursued the same policy. My dressing-gown was always ready; she followed after me to see if I needed any friendly office; she took it upon herself to represent me to strangers; she incensed me at times almost to madness. And yet for Hester's sake I must endure. I knew what that smooth smile portended, with the malice lying underneath. But I waited for the time when the touch of baby fingers would make my poor Hester forgetful of all else: then, I resolved, I would tell her every thing, and send Miriam away.

Dolly was my good angel through this trying period. Her sisterly kiss strengthened and heartened me, though I could see that she was very unhappy.

Twice she had met Ravaillac, — once in a cathedral, from which she came to me.

"He looked so wan and white!" she half sobbed. "It was a hot afternoon; and I had just come from the art school, feeling very tired, and almost ill. The heat overcame me, and I thought I should fall, when suddenly I saw the cool, dark interior of the old cathedral. Knowing that it was always open, I went in, walked up the wide, shadowed aisle checkered with dim blocks of color from the stained windows, and presently I went into a stately kind of pew, and there knelt down. When I looked up, somebody was kneeling beside me. I knew him in a moment, and my heart almost stood still. He turned, and looked at me. O Hal! I shall never forget that look!" she half sobbed, as she hid her tears on my shoulder.

"He didn't speak: he only looked. And presently he got up, moved reluctantly away, and went out of the cathedral, t — too m — much of a gen — gentleman to speak, unless I — gave — permission," she sobbed. From which I gathered that she would not have been very angry if he had spoken.

I met him myself not long after that; and the pallor of his face, the unnatural brilliancy of his eyes, shocked me.

"I really am very sorry for this thing, Ravaillac," I said. "If I could mend matters, I certainly would."

"It is of my own fault," he made reply, sadly; "but, my God! I cannot live without her. It is killing me!"

Not long after that, an item of painful interest was chronicled. Ravaillac was accidentally shot, so the newspaper report said, but the wound proved to be not dangerous. All these days Dolly moved round the rectory like a ghost, slowly, with pained eyes and parted lips. Only now and then she came and sat down beside me when I was reading, and I knew how she longed for comfort and companionship. Yet, when I essayed the former, she shrank from me; and so I found that silence suited her best. One day she came to me smiling, with the tears in her eyes.

"See, he has written to me," she said, "and you may read it."

She sat down, leaning her head on my shoulder while I read. My eye lighted on this paragraph.

"It was no chance shot: I deliberately tried to end my life. You, and you alone, shall know the truth. Since then, I am ashamed. God gave me the life which should be spent in his service. I have decided to go to my beloved country, alone — to live alone, and in works of mercy and charity try to forget. Forget! *mon Dieu*, never! But I will at least be a man!"

"There is more in Ravaillac than I thought," I said. "Don't you see it is the best thing he could do?"

"Oh! I suppose it is — he seems to think it best," she said in a very faint voice. "Yes, it is best, on the whole — for I suppose" — the increasing weight of her head upon my shoulder alarmed me. I looked round at Dolly. She had fainted.

CHAPTER XXIII.

*" A word fitly spoken,
How good it is!"*

THE next few months seemed marked with disaster. One of my wardens, a jolly, worldly fellow, — for we do not choose those officers because of ecclesiastical fitness, — came to me one day, wearing an absent expression so markedly foreign to his ordinary appearance, that I was anxious at once to know with what errand he had been charged, or had charged himself.

"To tell you the truth," he said in his brusque way, "I expect you will tell me to mind my own business, or perhaps pitch me out of the study. But I couldn't hear of these things, you know, and not go in. Why, I've had no end of rows on your account; and I'll be blamed if I don't knock down the next infernal rascal who dares to wag his tongue about you!"

My experience had prepared me to divine his meaning.

"I see," I said: " some of my parishioners

have been making a too free use of my name. I could tell you exactly what has been said. If they had come to me in the first place, I could easily have enlightened them; but they chose to stab me in the dark."

"I know it; and, after all, it's only a few of the mischief-makers, with Mrs. Stanley at the head, and Mrs. Dickory at the bottom."

"Ah! that woman, Mrs. Stanley, has never forgiven me."

"She never will, particularly as she has failed of her long-cherished purpose," was the rejoinder. "Tom Tracy has cut her dead, as the saying is. He has gone to the Epiphany, to sing; and she has no one to put on her shawl, or to tie her shoe-lacings if she wears 'em. I don't really, upon my soul, think Tom ever meant any harm. He's a queer fellow, is Tom; and, once suspected, his pride made it difficult, if not impossible, to give in: and my wife thinks, that if he had been a little less cold-natured, and had frankly admitted to his wife, that, as the people had been talking about him, he'd give 'em something to talk about, and let her see the curious and perhaps mixed motives that influenced him, she would not have died as she did. But Tom's a queer genius. Just speak of Tilly, and the tears will come in his eyes. Upon my soul, I believe the fellow thinks he was more sinned against than sinning. Lord! my wife knows, if I go down street for a pound of shingle-nails, what I'm going for. You see, I found out at first that it wouldn't do to have a divided household — reasoned it out on this plane. Man and wife are one, consequently I have no right to keep even matters of business from Liza. Tell you what, she has tided me over some mighty tough places, just because she knew when business went wrong. A fellow needn't put the full weight of his miseries and mistakes upon her; but it's best to go on the principle that a firm is bound to hold by each other, to retrench when necessary, to keep the balance-sheet correctly, and to have no secrets. That's what I call fair and square, and a man ain't half a man that don't do it."

I winced under the rude eloquence of my junior warden, though the humor of telling "Liza" made me smile. His wife was a little round woman, with the roses of sixteen and the smile of a baby; and she had never seemed to me like a woman who had a care in the world, or who could manage a household: while Hester was my ideal of a noble woman nobly planned, and yet I had shrunk from making her a confidante in so many cases where she could have aided me. I trembled when I thought of one, the most important business mistake I had ever made, and that threatened me in the near future with a serious loss. I had gone security for a man of whom, nearly a year before, Hester had expressed herself as distrustful, though anxious that I should aid him in his task of self-reform.

"Do what you can for him, but don't give him money," she had said. "He is bound to live on his friends."

Of course I had not told Hester; and I expected to find myself in that unfortunate position, where, my salary all taken to pay the debts of a dishonest man, as I found him to be, I must humiliate myself to make known my weakness in the character of a supplicant to my wife. How much better if I had asked, and acted upon, her advice!

"And they have gone so far as to say that somebody opened the door upon you in your study one day, and — well, I might as well out with it — found you with her arms about your neck."

I started from my chair.

"This is infernal!" I remembered the incident and Dolly's innocent caresses. Dear little Dolly! who only staid at the rectory for my sake; who was as much incensed against Miriam, for taking advantage of poor Hester's weakness and nervousness, as I could be, and who felt the gradual estrangement that seemed coming over Hester, almost as keenly as myself.

I told him the whole story, and threatened to resign.

"For Heaven's sake, don't think of such a thing!" said my friend. "This matter will right itself: leave it with me. I'm glad I know how it all came about, and I'll frighten Dickory and Company nearly out of their wits. Just leave it to me. Think no more about it; don't preach as if you noticed it; just go right on with your duties, and we'll have it all straightened out in a twinkling. You stick to the pulpit, and I'll stick to the preacher. There's only one of the vestry has lent an ear to this thing, and he would die if he didn't have a chance to suspect somebody. He made most of the trouble about Tom Tracy — though I don't defend Tom. Tom did wrong; and I think he sees it now, and would own it like a man. There's good in Tom, and I'm half sorry he was driven away; but there must be a storm now and then, I suppose, to clear the atmosphere: and ministers ain't no more exempt than other men, if they do live on a little higher plane than we folks in the pews. You see, they're expected to be such a super-angelic sort of persons, especially by the women-folks, that the least hint of a smudge leaves a black mark. Now, just don't you trouble yourself about it."

Indeed, I had neither the time nor the inclination to pursue the matter, and gladly left myself in the hands of my friends. Hester's increasing weakness alarmed me. She was so changed, that though I looked for a difference, even perhaps in mentality, I was not prepared to find my presence forbidden, with the knowledge conveyed to me by Miriam that my company was not at all times agreeable.

It was on one of these occasions that all the savage in me came to the surface; and, with a glance at the disturbing element that for the first time cowed her, I passed her, and went resolutely into the sitting-room of my wife.

She was very pale, but a delicate tinge of red touched her cheeks as she looked up from the depths of the great lounging-chair, which I had placed there with my own hands for her comfort. In her grasp was a daintily bound book, just from the press, Dolly's first literary venture of the kind; and her sewing lay by her side on a low table.

I kissed her: she did not return the kiss.

"Miriam said you were not so well, my darling," was my first remark, adding playfully, "that you didn't even wish to see me."

"Miriam was right," said Hester coldly; and my heart sank.

"What have I done, dear?" I ventured to ask.

"Oh!—nothing—except that you treat dear Miriam very unkindly—and—I—owe every thing to her!"

"Owe every thing to Miriam!—Miriam seems to be the motive-power in this household. I beg you to remember, Hester, that I have something to say in the matter, although I brought you nothing, and you brought me all. I am your husband, Hester!"

Her lips trembled, and her pallor increased.

"I am sorry you dislike my cousin so much: —there was a time—when"—she struggled violently to master her emotion. As in a lightning-flash, I saw it all revealed—the cruelty and perfidy of Miriam. What had she not told her? Hester had grown deadly pale. I put my arms out to infold her; but with a terrible cry she motioned me away, and then lay like one dead.

Then came the trial time,—a darkened house, stealthy footsteps, whispering voices, and finally the anguish of bending over a little image of my Hester, cold and white, beautiful as an angel, yet never to answer to love-words of mine, or of my poor, unconscious wife. For weeks Hester's life was despaired of: for months she was a helpless invalid, cared for by Miriam—always by Miriam.

I buried myself among my books. Dolly came in the study, and wrote beside me, night after night. We two were now, more than ever, all the world to each other. Miriam's beauty seemed sometimes almost unearthly in its demon-like quality. The blaze of gratified vengeance shone in her eyes. She took the reins in her own hands, and was virtually mistress of the house. Dolly and I talked it over, but we could come to no satisfactory conclusion. Even when Hester was pronounced out of danger, she received me with a stolid calm that shocked and shook me.

"Better to have followed her to the grave," I said to Dolly after one of these interviews. "My child is buried out of sight, and my wife is dead to me. What can be done?"

"It is all through Miriam," said Dolly. "Oh! how I hate falseness!" She shuddered. Poor little Dolly! she, too, was fighting her heart's battles, and finding her foes hard to conquer. "There is only one way," she said, after a little pause.

"And what is that?"

"Dismiss Miriam at once. I would not have counselled that before, but Hester is getting stronger. She will never be quite well, I think, till Miriam is gone."

"But how to do it? She will fly to Hester, disturb her peace, work upon her sympathy: in what way can I dismiss her? Hester is completely dominated, in her weak state, by Miriam's powerful will."

"You must not allow her to see Hester."

"She will. I can't lay hands on a woman, as I could if my opponent were a man, and put her out of the house."

"I think you can manage it," Dolly persisted. "I would."

"What plan have you thought of?" I queried, quite willing to be guided by a woman's judgment.

"I would lock the door the first evening she goes out, muffle or remove the door-bell, put her trunks outside, and have a carriage waiting at the gate, just as if she had arranged a journey. Her pride will not let her stay waiting long."

"But her belongings?"

"She keeps every thing in trunks. She is very much afraid of the servants; and all her things, with the exception of a few articles, are locked up. That is fortunate."

"But how will it sound abroad — that I turned my wife's cousin out of the house?"

"It will never be lisped. I know Miriam well enough for that. You have got to use harsh measures. Once she sees herself mastered and helpless, there is an end to it. The treacherous are seldom brave. She will not even seem to bear you malice, take my word for it."

"But where will she go?"

"What do you care where she goes? She has friends: let her use them. I have not a particle of pity for her. To think how she has abused your confidence, murdered your child"—

"Hush, Dolly!"

"It is simple truth," said Dolly. "You will have to win Hester all over again—but you can do it;" and she made a little triumphal flourish with her pen. "If Hester had been herself, this never would have happened, poor child! Now she only remembers the near past, and Miriam is a part of it. I really think, to save Hester's life, Miriam must go. Let us keep it all hidden in our hearts, and leave that woman to God. No one need ever know what she has been to us, or why she goes."

"Dolly, I believe you are a wise little counsellor," I said. "Hester may suffer less than we fear." The plan began to shape itself to my mind, and I took great delight in dwelling upon it. And this woman, who had plotted against my happiness, took holy communion from my hands, and drank the wine consecrated to believers!

I have often blessed God for the fact, strange as it may seem, that, among the twelve whose office was the regeneration of the world, a Judas was allowed to mingle his unholy ministrations.

It has kept my faith when I have seen the offices of our holy religion made subservient to greed and lust and hypocrisy. There be saints and saints; and if you will give me a hearty, whole-souled sinner — reputedly — in the place of some of these latter, I shall preach the gospel to better acceptance.

CHAPTER XXIV.

*" At last the peace of perfect love,
No doubt our rest disturbing."*

DOLLY and I held our peace like the couple of conspirators we were, only now and then Dolly begged me to try and seem more natural.

"One would think you were plotting terrible things," she said, "while in reality you are only saving your family peace by using a little strategy."

"I cannot appear at my ease where Miriam is," was my answer. "I shall never draw a happy breath till she is clean gone. But she never goes out."

"Oh! the time will come," said Dolly; "be patient. I know she will go out some evening this week, when her cousin is asleep, and 'must not be disturbed.' I can hear her say it. She would not leave her alone while awake, for the world."

The time did come. There was to be a service; but, luckily, Dolly did not attend church that evening: and equally lucky was it, that a young ministerial brother visited me in my study, and consented to take my place. Dolly came to the study-door with the glad news just as the bell was tolling; and I excused myself to my friend, and hurried into the house. In less than an hour Miriam's trunks were set out in the yard, the service was over, the church and rectory locked, and a coachman standing at the gate-entrance, to be paid by the hour, even if he staid there all night.

Dolly and I remained in the front parlor till the veiled figure of Miriam came up the walk, and paused at the strange sight that met her gaze. Then she mounted the steps, and rang the door-bell. No sound. The bell was carefully muffled, as it had been many and many a day of her evil ministration, when her victim lay unconscious, and apparently dying.

At last she seemed to comprehend that she was out-generalled. She stood irresolute for a moment, ran down the steps, mounted them again, made a gesture of superb disdain, and, as Dolly had conjectured she would, submitted to the inevitable with the best grace she could; and presently the carriage rolled away, and a great load of care rolled off my heart. Once more home was home! Oh, how happy I felt moving through the pleasant rooms with Dolly by my side! Never should that woman step over the threshold of my door again. All the evil of our human nature seemed to me personified in that evil, beautiful figure and face. The very recollection of her gifts and graces kindled me to wrath. Hester was no longer to be divided in her affection, her care, her duties; she was all mine: and the old love came up in my heart, like a flame newly kindled, as I crept up-stairs, only to look upon Hester's thin white face as she slept.

Poor child! she was but the shadow of her former self. Her hand, resting on the white cover; her cheek, rivalling the pillow in whiteness; the long, thick lashes casting a heavy shadow on the pallor beneath them; her pretty, childlike lips parted, and her teeth glistening in the dim light — how my heart ached as I thought of all she had suffered!

She stirred a little as I stood there, — I hoped she would wake, — and from her lips came a moan; but it sounded like "Miriam," and I turned away.

What a sense of triumph was mine as the memories of the past crowded thickly upon my brain! I was master now, alike of my home and my wife, — master, I mean, in the sense of possession only.

I moved a step farther, and the hot tears

rushed to my eyes as they fell on the beautiful little cradle that I had purchased after days of search for something fitting for such a treasure. There it stood, pure white, its canopy edged with costly lace, its silken cover pitifully smooth and straight. And there beside it was the dainty baby-basket, all the work of Hester's fingers, but every thing as polished, as perfect, as intact, as the day she finished her pretty work "for baby."

It was with real heart-ache I turned away, and sought my own room, that looked no longer cheerless and deserted, but filled with a dream-like presence.

In the morning the delightful consciousness flowed in upon me with the first sense of daylight and sunshine, that the hated incubus was gone. Heretofore I had dawdled over every duty: now my fingers flew. I longed to get down-stairs, and throw all the house open. Dolly met me. She had been up in Hester's room, and looked a little grave.

"Of course there were many things to do," she said, " and Miriam was a good nurse. Hester was astonished, and asked for *her* as soon as I came in. I told her Miriam had gone the night before, and had not yet returned. Would I do? She used to like to have me comb her hair. No, she would wait for Miriam.

Meantime I knew what was always prepared for her breakfast; and, when the time came, I carried it up-stairs. Hester was nervous, and a little irritable; couldn't imagine what had come over Miriam. But she took her chocolate and oatmeal, and ate a little. Then she allowed me to arrange her hair, but seemed very thoughtful. All at once she threw her hands up, saying, —

"'I see it! I see it all! you have sent Miriam away. You were meanly jealous of the poor child, and I shall never see her again.'

"With that she just fell over on the pillow, and began to cry, and beg Miriam to come back, till I was frightened. I left her that way. What is to be done now? I have been asking myself whether you had better go up and try to soothe her. We shall have her ill again."

What would be the end of this complication of affairs, it was difficult to foresee. Hester was so changed and so weak from her long illness, that it was perhaps as much as her life was worth to cross her now; and I hardly knew what to do. It is a curious situation for a man to be in, when he dares not venture into the presence of his own wife, or goes there with fear and trembling, as I did.

Opening the door, I saw that Hester was still prostrate with grief, and lay there softly sobbing.

"Hester!" I said.

She did not move, only buried her face deeper in the pillow.

"My dear little wife!"

I took her fingers, but she threw my grasp aside; and for some time I sat there in silence, anxious and perplexed.

"Can this be the dear girl that I married?" I asked softly.

She lifted herself, her eyes ablaze, the crimson of fever in her cheeks.

"Yes, yes! you married *me* — but you *loved* Miriam Hope! O Hal! how could you be so cruel? How dared you?"

For the moment I was utterly incapable of reply. My heart beat heavily, and I could feel its pulsations all over my body. Such an extraordinary assertion! so utterly false! and from Hester's lips! What damning evidence had Miriam given to justify such language and such defiance? What had not my wife suffered? my poor darling! With all my anger, I pitied her.

"What has that woman been telling you, Hester?" I asked, after a pause, as calmly as I could.

"All your falseness, your duplicity — your cruelty — and you a minister of Christ!"

Her words went straight to my heart.

"If *I* had only told you all!" I groaned.

"What! there is worse?" she cried with a look of horror.

"No, Hester: there is no crime on my soul, unless it be that of having loved my wife too well," I made reply. And then, made eloquent by the exigency of the circumstances, I poured out my whole heart. I told her every thing, — of my weakness, not infidelity; of my want of true manhood, my vanity; of Miriam's duplicity, her confessions, her recriminations, — till the tables were turned, and I had proved it was I who suffered, who had been wronged. When Hester saw all, — and she did, — I had won my wife back. When she saw all, she saw treason and treachery of the blackest. She saw that her life had been poisoned at the very fountain-head by her cousin's baseness, and her little babe paid with its life the penalty of her own rash credence. Not for worlds would she have had Miriam back.

"Oh, it has been such a night of horrors!" she said, her dear head resting in its olden place upon my bosom. "But you will forgive me — we shall be happy again?"

"Yes," I made reply, "now that our home is purified, and my wife has come back to me."

"O Hal! and I tried to think I hated you," she sobbed.

It seemed as if that were a day of wonders.

Dolly brought me a letter written in the quaintest English, which proved to be from the old grandmother of Mr. Ravaillac. It besought Dolly to have pity on her grandson, the dear child of her old age, who was, ah! so unhappy, so wretched, so penitent, and who had confessed all to her. She spoke in terms most eloquent of his goodness to her, his virtues, his tenderness, and ended by an allusion to their family name, which was old, and had been famous, though they had no escutcheon of nobility.

"Shall you answer it, dear?" I asked.

"I — think I will," she said, smiling. "You see, I have been in correspondence with — *him* — since he went to France — just friendly letters — and — well, he is coming back to America."

I kissed Dolly, for I was very glad.

I am still at old St. John's. My people love me. I have buried their dead, married their children, visited their poor, sick, and dying, for the last ten years. Many of the old people have passed to their long home. Many of the younger have moved to other places. Of those who remain, Mrs. Dickory still files into church with her train of children, in all eight or nine, and performs the most unaccountable antics all through service and sermon. But I have only to raise my eyes to see two golden heads, my own blue-eyed darlings, Hester seven, Dolly five, who sit so demurely, hiding all their little rogues'-tricks under the prim bonnets and pretty Sunday garments, and I forget Mrs. Dickory and the Dickory brood.

Tom Tracy has come back, repentant, into the fold of the church; and he sings as delightfully as when in the old days he vexed the souls of the righteous, even as he drew their hearts out with his marvellously sweet voice.

Marguerite is away at school, and never hints now of her visions or fantasies, if such they were. For myself, I am not prepared to decide.

Miriam married a very good man, but there is a rumor in the air that she is not happy; and we have lately learned that there was insanity in the Hope family, which accounts in a measure for her wayward fancies and strange moods. We seldom meet.

Ravaillac is on his way to Paris for the third time since his marriage. Dolly goes with him every voyage, and comes back to us radiant. She is a happy little woman; and, if there is any moral in my story, it is summed up in the title of this little book, —

TELL YOUR WIFE.

MARY A. DENISON'S NOVELS.

UNIFORM EDITION. CLOTH, $1; PAPER, 50 CENTS.

HIS TRIUMPH.

"A sprightly story is 'His Triumph,' in spite of the fact that it opens with a wedding, and ends with a renunciation. We read of two runaways, of lovers' letters, of a haunted house, a *debutante*, and all of the romance and reality that pertain to a well-conceived and well-told story. Mrs. Denison is a skilful story-teller, and 'His Triumph' is also her triumph." — *Philadelphia Keystone.*

LIKE A GENTLEMAN.

"The story of one who drank 'like a gentleman' is one of Mrs. Denison's best stories. The lovers of romance will pronounce this story charming, and be all the more pleased with it because some of the characters are purer, sweeter, and nobler than are often found in real life. The incidents are thrilling, the plot interesting, the story well told."

ROTHMELL.

"The style is clear and bright, abounding in little novel pictures and delicate touches. Rothmell, the principal hero, is a brilliant surgeon, with a magnetic eye, but a penchant in earlier life for marrying rich women, which, indulged in, gives him considerable after trouble." — *Chicago Inter-Ocean.*

THAT WIFE OF MINE.

"There is now and then a touch of genuine pathos. Its incidents, its characters, its language, are of the every-day sort: but its very simplicity and naturalness give it a charm to the ordinary reader; and it is undeniably pure and healthful in its tone. We must pronounce 'That Wife of Mine' an excellent book of its kind." — *Boston Journal.*

THAT HUSBAND OF MINE.

"It is as bright and cheery as a sunbeam. Sparkles like dewdrops. Full of good humor, with a great deal of patience. It teaches you how to get a husband, how to manage one, and how an engagement can be broken. It will amuse you and make you laugh. After reading the first page, you will feel like joining in the pursuit of 'That Husband of Mine.'"

MR. PETER CREWITT.

"'Peter Crewitt,' from the same house, is a Dickens-sort of a story. ... There are passages of pathos, of moralizing, of pointed ridicule and satire, that would do credit to the ablest novelist. The average novel-reader will become quite infatuated over 'Peter Crewitt.'" — *Advertiser*, Elmira, N.Y.

Sold by all booksellers and newsdealers, and sent by mail, postpaid, on receipt of price.

LEE AND SHEPARD, Publishers, Boston.

THE DOUGLAS NOVELS.
By Miss Amanda M. Douglas.

Uniform Volumes.   *Price $1.50 each.*

A WOMAN'S INHERITANCE.
"Like all the romances of Miss Douglas, this story has a fascination about it which enchains the reader's attention until the end." — *Baltimore News.*

OUT OF THE WRECK; or, was it a Victory?
"Bright and entertaining as Miss Douglas's stories always are, this, her new one, leads them all." — *New-Bedford Standard.*

FLOYD GRANDON'S HONOR.
"Fascinating throughout, and worthy of the reputation of the author." — *Philadelphia Methodist.*

WHOM KATHIE MARRIED.
Kathie was the heroine of the popular series of Kathie Stories for young people, the readers of which were very anxious to know with whom Kathie settled down in life. Hence this story, charmingly written.

LOST IN A GREAT CITY.
"There is the power of delineation and robustness of expression that would credit a masculine hand in the present volume, and the reader will at no stage of the reading regret having commenced its perusal. In some parts it is pathetic, even to eloquence." — *San Francisco Post.*

THE OLD WOMAN WHO LIVED IN A SHOE.
"The romances of Miss Douglas's creation are all thrillingly interesting." — *Cambridge Tribune.*

HOPE MILLS; or, Between Friend and Sweetheart.
"Amanda Douglas is one of the favorite authors of American novel-readers." — *Manchester Mirror.*

FROM HAND TO MOUTH.
"There is real satisfaction in reading this book, from the fact that we can so readily 'take it home' to ourselves." — *Portland Argus.*

NELLY KINNARD'S KINGDOM.
"The Hartford Religious Herald" says, "This story is so fascinating, that one can hardly lay it down after taking it up."

IN TRUST; or, Dr. Bertrand's Household.
"She writes in a free, fresh, and natural way; and her characters are never overdrawn." — *Manchester Mirror.*

CLAUDIA.
"The plot is very dramatic, and the *dénoûment* startling. Claudia, the heroine, is one of those self-sacrificing characters which it is the glory of the female sex to produce." — *Boston Journal.*

STEPHEN DANE.
"This is one of this author's happiest and most successful attempts at novel-writing, for which a grateful public will applaud her." — *Herald.*

HOME NOOK; or, the Crown of Duty.
"An interesting story of home-life, not wanting in incident, and written in forcible and attractive style." — *New-York Graphic.*

SYDNIE ADRIANCE; or, Trying the World.
"The works of Miss Douglas have stood the test of popular judgment, and become the fashion. They are true, natural in delineation, pure and elevating in their tone." — *Express, Easton, Penn.*

SEVEN DAUGHTERS.
The charm of the story is the perfectly natural and home-like air which pervades it.

Sold by all booksellers, and sent by mail, postpaid, on receipt of price.

J. T. TROWBRIDGE'S NOVELS.
NEW UNIFORM EDITION.

FARNELL'S FOLLY.

"As a Novel of American Society, this book has never been surpassed. Hearty in style and wholesome in tone. Its pathos often melting to tears, its humor always exciting merriment."

CUDJO'S CAVE.

Like "Uncle Tom's Cabin," this thrilling story was a stimulating power in the civil war, and had an immense sale. Secretary Chase, of President Lincoln's cabinet, said of it, "I could not help reading it: it interested and impressed me profoundly."

THE THREE SCOUTS.

Another popular book of the same stamp, of which "The Boston Transcript" said, "It promises to have a larger sale than 'Cudjo's Cave.' It is impossible to open the volume at any page without being struck by the quick movement and pervading anecdote of the story."

THE DRUMMER BOY.

A Story of Burnside's Expedition. Illustrated by F. O. C. DARLEY.

"The most popular book of the season. It will sell without pushing." — *Zion's Herald.*

MARTIN MERRIVALE: His X Mark.

"Strong in humor, pathos, and unabated interest. In none of the books issued from the American press can there be found a purer or more delicate sentiment, a more genuine good taste, or a nicer appreciation and brighter delineation of character." — *English Journal.*

NEIGHBOR JACKWOOD.

A story of New-England life in the slave-tracking days. Dramatized for the Boston Museum, it had a long run to crowded houses. The story is one of Trowbridge's very best.

COUPON BONDS, and other Stories.

The leading story is undoubtedly the most popular of Trowbridge's short stories. The others are varied in character, but are either intensely interesting or "highly amusing."

NEIGHBORS' WIVES.

An ingenious and well-told story. Two neighbors' wives are tempted beyond their strength to resist, and steal each from the other. One is discovered in the act, under ludicrous and humiliating circumstances, but is generously pardoned, with a promise of secrecy. Of course she betrays her secret, and of course perplexities come. It is a capital story.

12mo. Cloth. Price per volume, $1.50.

Sold by all booksellers and newsdealers, and sent by mail, postpaid, on receipt of price.

MISS VIRGINIA F. TOWNSEND'S BOOKS.

Uniform Edition. Cloth. $1.50 Each.

BUT A PHILISTINE.

"Another novel by the author of 'A Woman's Word' and 'Lenox Dare,' will be warmly welcomed by hosts of readers of Miss Townsend's stories. There is nothing of the 'sensational,' or so-called realistic, school in her writings. On the contrary, they are noted for their healthy moral tone and pure sentiment, and yet are not wanting in STRIKING SITUATIONS AND DRAMATIC INCIDENTS." — *Chicago Journal.*

LENOX DARE.

"Her stories, always sunny and healthful, touch the springs of social life, and make the reader better acquainted with this great human organization of which we all form a part, and tend to bring him into more intimate sympathy with what is most pure and noble in our nature. Among the best of her productions we place the volume here under notice. In temper and tone the volume is calculated to exert a healthful and elevating influence." — *New-England Methodist.*

DARYLL GAP; or, Whether it Paid.

A story of the petroleum days, and of a family who struck oil.

"Miss Townsend is a very entertaining writer, and, while she entertains, at the same time instructs. Her plots are well arranged, and her characters are clearly and strongly drawn. The present volume will not detract from the reputation she has heretofore enjoyed." — *Pittsburg Recorder.*

A WOMAN'S WORD, AND HOW SHE KEPT IT.

"The celebrity of Virginia F. Townsend as an authoress, her brilliant descriptive powers, and pure, vigorous imagination, will insure a hearty welcome for the above-entitled volume in the writer's happiest vein. Every woman will understand the self-sacrifice of Genevieve Weir, and will entertain only scorn for the miserable man who imbittered her life to hide his own wrong-doing."—*Fashion Quarterly.*

THAT QUEER GIRL.

"A fresh, wholesome book about good men and good women, bright and cheery in style, and pure in morals. Just the book to take a young girl's fancy, and help her to grow up, like Madeline and Argia, into the sweetness of real girlhood; there being more of that same sweetness under the fuss and feathers of the present day than a casual observer might suppose."— *People's Monthly.*

ONLY GIRLS.

"This volume shows how two persons, 'only girls,' saved two men from crime, even from ruin of body and soul; and all this came about in their lives without their purpose or knowledge at the time, and not at all as they or anybody else would have planned it; but it comes about well and naturally enough. The story is ingenious and graphic, and kept the writer of this notice up far into the small hours of yesterday morning." — *Washington Chronicle.*

Sold by all booksellers and newsdealers, and sent by mail, postpaid, on receipt of price.

LEE & SHEPARD, Publishers, Boston.

SOPHIE MAY'S "GROWN-UP" BOOKS.

Uniform Binding. All Handsomely Illustrated. $1.50.

JANET, A POOR HEIRESS.

"The heroine of this story is a true girl. An imperious, fault-finding, unappreciative father alienates her love, and nearly ruins her temper. The mother knows the father is at fault, but does not dare to say so. Then comes a discovery, that she is only an adopted daughter; a forsaking of the old home; a life of strange vicissitudes; a return; a marriage under difficulties; and a discovery, that, after all, she is an heiress. The story is certainly a very attractive one." — *Chicago Interior.*

THE DOCTOR'S DAUGHTER.

"Sophie May, author of the renowned Prudy and Dotty books, has achieved another triumph in the new book with this title just issued. She has taken 'a new departure' this time, and written a new story for grown-up folks. If we are not much mistaken, the young folks will want to read it, as much as the old folks want to read the books written for the young ones. It is a splendid story for all ages." — *Lynn Semi-Weekly Recorder.*

THE ASBURY TWINS.

"The announcement of another work by this charming and popular writer will be heartily welcomed by the public. And in this sensible, fascinating story of the twin-sisters, 'Vic' and 'Van,' they have before them a genuine treat. Vic writes her story in one chapter, and Van in the next, and so on through the book. Van is frank, honest, and practical; Vic wild, venturesome, and witty; and both of them natural and winning. At home or abroad, they are true to their individuality, and see things with their own eyes. It is a fresh, delightful volume, well worthy of its gifted author." — *Boston Contributor.*

OUR HELEN.

"'Our Helen' is Sophie May's latest creation; and she is a bright, brave girl, that the young people will all like. We are pleased to meet with some old friends in the book. It is a good companion-book for the 'Doctor's Daughter,' and the two should go together. Queer old Mrs. O'Neil still lives, to indulge in the reminiscences of the young men of Machias; and other Quinnebasset people with familiar names occasionally appear, along with new ones who are worth knowing. 'Our Helen' is a noble and unselfish girl, but with a mind and will of her own; and the contrast between her and pretty, fascinating, selfish little Sharley, is very finely drawn. Lee & Shepard publish it." — *Holyoke Transcript.*

QUINNEBASSET GIRLS.

"The story is a very attractive one, as free from the sensational and impossible as could be desired, and at the same time full of interest, and pervaded by the same bright, cheery sunshine that we find in the author's earlier books. She is to be congratulated on the success of her essay in a new field of literature, to which she will be warmly welcomed by those who know and admire her 'Prudy Books.'"

Sold by all booksellers and newsdealers, and sent by mail, postpaid, on receipt of price.

LEE & SHEPARD, Publishers, Boston.

Lee and Shepard's Books of Travel.

GERMANY SEEN WITHOUT SPECTACLES; or, Random Sketches of Various Subjects, Penned from Different Stand-points in the Empire. By HENRY RUGGLES, late U. S. Consul at the Island of Malta, and at Barcelona, Spain. $1.50.

"Mr. Ruggles writes briskly: he chats and gossips, slashing right and left with stout American prejudices, and has made withal a most entertaining book." — *New-York Tribune.*

TRAVELS AND OBSERVATIONS IN THE ORIENT, with a Hasty Flight in the Countries of Europe. By WALTER HARRIMAN (ex-Governor of New Hampshire). $1.50.

"The author, in his graphic description of these sacred localities, refers with great aptness to scenes and personages which history has made famous. It is a chatty narrative of travel, tinged throughout with a very natural and pleasant color of personality." — *Concord Monitor.*

FORE AND AFT. A Story of Actual Sea-Life. By ROBERT B. DIXON, M.D. $1.25.

Travels in Mexico, with vivid descriptions of manners and customs, form a large part of this striking narrative of a fourteen-months' voyage.

VOYAGE OF THE PAPER CANOE. A Geographical Journey of Twenty-five Hundred Miles from Quebec to the Gulf of Mexico. By NATHANIEL H. BISHOP. With numerous Illustrations and maps specially prepared for this work. Crown 8vo. $1.50.

"Mr. Bishop did a very bold thing, and has described it with a happy mixture of spirit, keen observation, and *bonhomie.*" — *London Graphic.*

FOUR MONTHS IN A SNEAK-BOX. A Boat-Voyage of Twenty-six Hundred Miles down the Ohio and Mississippi Rivers, and along the Gulf of Mexico. By NATHANIEL H. BISHOP. With numerous maps and illustrations. $1.50.

"His glowing pen-pictures of 'shanty-boat' life on the great rivers are true to life. His descriptions of persons and places are graphic." — *Zion's Herald.*

A THOUSAND MILES' WALK ACROSS SOUTH AMERICA, Over the Pampas and the Andes. By NATHANIEL H. BISHOP. Crown 8vo. New Edition. Illustrated. $1.50.

"Mr. Bishop made this journey when a boy of sixteen, has never forgotten it, and tells it in such a way that the reader will always remember it, and wish there had been more."

CAMPS IN THE CARIBBEES. Being the Adventures of a Naturalist Bird-Hunting in the West-India Islands. By FRED A. OBER. Crown 8vo. With maps and illustrations. $2.50.

"During two years he visited mountains, forests, and people that few, if any, tourists had ever reached before. He carried his camera with him, and photographed from nature the scenes by which the book is illustrated." — *Louisville Courier-Journal.*

Sold by all booksellers, and sent by mail, postpaid, on receipt of price.

LEE & SHEPARD, Publishers, Boston.

LEE AND SHEPARD'S BOOKS OF TRAVEL.

LIFE AT PUGET SOUND. With sketches of travel in Washington Territory, British Columbia, Oregon, and California. By CAROLINE C. LEIGHTON. 16mo. Cloth. $1.50.

"Your chapters on Puget Sound have charmed me. Full of life, deeply interesting, and with just that class of facts, and suggestions of truth, that cannot fail to help the Indian and the Chinese." — WENDELL PHILLIPS.

EUROPEAN BREEZES. By MARGERY DEANE. Cloth. Gilt top. $1.50. Being chapters of travel through Germany, Austria, Hungary, and Switzerland, covering places not usually visited by Americans in making "The Grand Tour of the Continent," by the accomplished writer of "Newport Breezes."

"A very bright, fresh, and amusing account, which tells us about a host of things we never heard of before, and is worth two ordinary books on European travel." — *Woman's Journal.*

AN AMERICAN GIRL ABROAD. By Miss ADELINE TRAFTON, author of "His Inheritance," "Katherine Earle," etc. 16mo. Illustrated. $1.50.

"A sparkling account of a European trip by a wide-awake, intelligent, and irrepressible American girl. Pictured with a freshness and vivacity that is delightful." — *Utica Observer.*

BEATEN PATHS; or, A Woman's Vacation in Europe. By ELLA W. THOMPSON. 16mo. Cloth. $1.50.

A lively and chatty book of travel, with pen-pictures humorous and graphic, that are decidedly out of the "beaten paths" of description.

A SUMMER IN THE AZORES, with a Glimpse of Madeira. By Miss C. ALICE BAKER. Little Classic style. Cloth. Gilt edges. $1.25.

"Miss Baker gives us a breezy, entertaining description of these picturesque islands. She is an observing traveller, and makes a graphic picture of the quaint people and customs." — *Chicago Advance.*

ENGLAND FROM A BACK WINDOW; With Views of Scotland and Ireland. By J. M. BAILEY, the "'Danbury News' Man." 12mo. $1.50.

"The peculiar humor of this writer is well known. The British Isles have never before been looked at in just the same way, — at least, not by any one who has notified us of the fact. Mr. Bailey's travels possess, accordingly, a value of their own for the reader, no matter how many previous records of journeys in the mother country he may have read." — *Rochester Express.*

OVER THE OCEAN; or, Sights and Scenes in Foreign Lands. By CURTIS GUILD, editor of "The Boston Commercial Bulletin." Crown 8vo. Cloth, $2.50.

"The utmost that any European tourist can hope to do is to tell the old story in a somewhat fresh way, and Mr. Guild has succeeded in every part of his book in doing this." — *Philadelphia Bulletin.*

ABROAD AGAIN; or, Fresh Forays in Foreign Fields. Uniform with "Over the Ocean." By the same author. Crown 8vo. Cloth, $2.50.

"He has given us a life-picture. Europe is done in a style that must serve as an invaluable guide to those who go 'over the ocean,' as well as an interesting companion." — *Halifax Citizen.*

Sold by all booksellers, and sent by mail, postpaid, on receipt of price.

LEE & SHEPARD, Publishers, Boston.

TROPHIES OF TRAVEL.

DRIFTING ROUND THE WORLD; A Boy's Adventures by Sea and Land. By CAPT. CHARLES W. HALL, author of "Adrift in the Ice-Fields," "The Great Bonanza," etc. With numerous full-page and letter-press illustrations. Royal 8vo. Handsome cover. $1.75. Cloth. Gilt. $2.50.

"Out of the beaten track" in its course of travel, record of adventures, and descriptions of life in Greenland, Labrador, Ireland, Scotland, England, France, Holland, Russia, Asia, Siberia, and Alaska. Its hero is young, bold, and adventurous; and the book is in every way interesting and attractive.

EDWARD GREÉY'S JAPANESE SERIES.

YOUNG AMERICANS IN JAPAN; or, The Adventures of the Jewett Family and their Friend Oto Nambo. With 170 full-page and letter-press illustrations. Royal 8vo, 7 x 9¼ inches. Handsomely illuminated cover. $1.75. Cloth, black and gold, $2.50.

This story, though essentially a work of fiction, is filled with interesting and truthful descriptions of the curious ways of living of the good people of the land of the rising sun.

THE WONDERFUL CITY OF TOKIO; or, The Further Adventures of the Jewett Family and their Friend Oto Nambo. With 169 illustrations. Royal 8vo, 7 x 9¼ inches. With cover in gold and colors, designed by the author. $1.75. Cloth, black and gold, $2.50.

"A book full of delightful information. The author has the happy gift of permitting the reader to view things as he saw them. The illustrations are mostly drawn by a Japanese artist, and are very unique." — *Chicago Herald.*

THE BEAR WORSHIPPERS OF YEZO AND THE ISLAND OF KARAFUTO; being the further Adventures of the Jewett Family and their Friend Oto Nambo. 180 illustrations. Boards. $1.75. Cloth, $2.50.

Graphic pen and pencil pictures of the remarkable bearded people who live in the north of Japan. The illustrations are by native Japanese artists, and give queer pictures of a queer people, who have been seldom visited.

HARRY W. FRENCH'S BOOKS.

OUR BOYS IN INDIA. The wanderings of two young Americans in Hindustan, with their exciting adventures on the sacred rivers and wild mountains. With 145 illustrations. Royal 8vo, 7 x 9¼ inches. Bound in emblematic covers of Oriental design, $1.75. Cloth, black and gold, $2.50.

While it has all the exciting interest of a romance, it is remarkably vivid in its pictures of manners and customs in the land of the Hindu. The illustrations are many and excellent.

OUR BOYS IN CHINA. The adventures of two young Americans, wrecked in the China Sea on their return from India, with their strange wanderings through the Chinese Empire. 188 illustrations. Boards, ornamental covers in colors and gold. $1.75. Cloth, $2.50.

This gives the further adventures of "Our Boys" of India fame in the land of Teas and Queues.

Sold by all booksellers, and sent by mail, postpaid, on receipt of price.

LEE & SHEPARD, Publishers, Boston.

www.ingramcontent.com/pod-product-compliance
Lightning Source LLC
Chambersburg PA
CBHW021410230426
43666CB00006B/696